My Sailing Life

by

Peter J Faulkner

For Jacquie

My best friend, adventurous companion and love of my life.

<u>Acknowledgements</u>

Many thanks to these wonderful people:

Alison Ringer and Jean Faulkner for your proofreading and advice.

Jamie, Sam and our family and friends, who have been so supportive of this challenging project.

Jacquie Rodewald
for the endless hours typing, rearranging and listening.

Contents

Prologue

The line ripped through the water at a great rate of knots and was stripped off the reel with the ratchet screaming. The rod was in a harness and within a minute we had lost at least 200 yards of line, so this was one big fish. I knew straight away it wasn't a yellowfin or a bigeye tuna, as we had caught them before. This was something much larger.

It dived really deep and my older brother Mike skilfully manoeuvred the boat backwards to take the strain off. I quickly increased the drag on the reel, trying to slow the fish down without breaking the line. The rod was bent double and I kept pumping back and forth to get some more line in, but that fish was not cooperating and was still stripping line off at an alarming rate. After about half an hour I managed to reel it in a bit more and I could feel that the fish was starting to tire.

We fought that fish for over an hour until it finally leapt out of the water. It was a spectacular fish – a southern bluefin tuna – one of the most valuable fish on the Japanese market.

It was 1968 and I had just turned 17, so it was very exciting to crew for Mike during the school holidays. He was skippering a commercial fishing boat for a local company so it had a heavy hydraulic gantry and harness for landing big fish without damaging them. We knew certain types of fish could attract high prices at the Tokyo Fish Market if they looked perfect, so we had to handle this fish carefully.

That tuna was by far the biggest I've ever seen and I was stunned by its beauty when we first pulled it out of the sea. The fish was trying to thrash wildly but it was tired and the harness held, so we killed it quickly with the iki spike and swung it inboard into a fish hold full of ice.

The tuna was six feet two inches long and around 450 pounds, so we didn't need to catch anything else and headed straight back to the harbour. It was caught on a lure that we were trailing behind the boat and we deliberately left the lure in its mouth to show that it was not caught on a longline.

Mike radioed ahead to book a flight leaving Gisborne in an hour with a connection from Auckland to Tokyo. The fish would have a three-hour wait in Auckland but would stay chilled in its bed of ice inside a huge insulated container.

This was a very exciting moment for both of us, as it would be the first time Mike had ever attempted to get a fish to the Tokyo markets. The auction would be held there the following morning.

Our tuna must have arrived in perfect condition and we were absolutely amazed to learn that it sold for $62,120 – one of the top prices of the day. The boat owners and Mike each received 40 percent. Expenses such as fuel, boat maintenance and flights took 10 percent. Most importantly, as crew, I received 10 percent. That meant I banked $6000 – not bad for a high school student on a weekly allowance of one dollar.

It was our first and last foray into the lucrative Japanese market, and, when I crewed for Mike on subsequent trips, I made very little. It

was just as well I enjoyed fishing regardless of
the income.

Chapter One

The unique seaweed smell of the sea, the pressure of wind on sail and the feel of the waves against the hull were making a huge impression on me.

My first sailing experience was on a Herreshoff 28, owned by my brother Mike's friend, Tony Sayers. It was January 1970 in Poverty Bay, near Gisborne on the east coast of New Zealand.

I had been to sea many times before, on board my father's fishing vessel at the age of eight and later as crew on my brother Mike's commercial fishing boats.

The difference between motor and sail made an impression I will never forget. There is something special about the way a yacht heels over and surges ahead with each gust of wind, so quietly that all you can hear is the rigging creaking and the water swishing past the hull.

It got into my blood. I'm not sure how it gets in there, but it certainly can't be got out. That sailing experience lasted only a few hours, but it changed my life quite dramatically.

Six years later, I had passed my New Zealand Certificate of Science in biology, while working at the Department of Scientific and Industrial Research in Palmerston North. I'm not sure how I passed, as I had so many other distractions. I was singing in a band that had just finished performing on a cruise ship around the world. I also belonged to five different clubs, so I was spreading myself pretty thinly.

I talked to lots of people about yachts, and it seemed the more they said I couldn't build one, the more determined I became to do it. The decision seemed to be making itself. I would build an ocean-going yacht, but what should it be built of and what size and which rig was best: modern fin keel or traditional long keel, ketch or cutter? Could I really build one? How long would it take and could I afford it? It seemed I had a lot of unanswered questions.

I thought a lot about the merits of building or renovating a house, instead, as I knew I could make more money out of that, while building a yacht meant all my assets would be at risk, as international insurance was too expensive. The more I thought about it, the closer I came to the conclusion that the adventure and challenge of building and sailing a yacht was what was driving me on.

Weeks of research followed and finally some decisions were made. She would be approximately 35 feet and built of steel, with a full length keel and transom-hung rudder.

Why? Firstly, 35 feet seemed to be the smallest size that would perform satisfactorily with the weight of steel and still give plenty of storage and living space. It was cheaper and stronger than wood or fibreglass and steel was also the easiest medium for an amateur to build a sturdy boat – a big factor when sailing among coral reefs.

It was time to decide what to do next. Should I continue studying for an academic career in science or build a yacht and sail away? The latter seemed an impossible dream.

How or why the dream became reality, I've no idea, but one thing was certain. I needed a substantial challenge.

The next step was learning those building skills. Night school welding lessons would take too long, so I approached a few engineering companies for a welding job, as that seemed the only way to learn quickly.

After being turned down by three companies, I spoke to the owner of McIntosh Bros Engineering, who I had heard was into boating. I didn't hold out much hope of success, but, when I told him I wanted to build a steel yacht, he was extremely interested.

After talking a lot about boats, I finally had a welding job: 10 hours a day for a month making rubbish skips, which were the same steel plate thickness as my yacht would be. After being told that my welding looked like bird shit and would leak like a sieve, I couldn't work out what I was doing wrong.

I picked the brains of the best welder in the company and soon I was producing some good results. It was merely a matter of the right heat, holding the welding rod at the right angle, the distance of the rod from the steel and a few other techniques. At the end of 200 hours welding and fabricating, I could finally build a rubbish skip that would float.

I managed to secure a corner of an industrial section in Palmerston North for the princely sum of one dollar per week.

A large house was being demolished nearby and they had no use for the old four-by-two frames and corrugated iron, so I was able to build a large shed for almost nothing. Prior to that, I hadn't done any building, apart from a little bird aviary in my mother's backyard.

The owner of the industrial section called round to have a look and saw for the first time the huge rusty monstrosity I'd built on his tidy section. He was shocked, as it was a bit of an eyesore. I managed to placate him by promising it would only be there for about six months, by which time I would be able to pull it down and continue building the boat without it. I learned early in life that it was much easier to ask for forgiveness than for permission.

A major step in building a yacht is "lofting" the plans from small-scale paper plans to full size plans on sheets of plywood. Colin Childs, the designer of the revenue cutter I was building, agreed to drive from Auckland to Palmerston North for the weekend. We drafted the frames, stem bar and transom into full scale plans.

In complete awe of the task ahead, I didn't know where to start, so I decided to dive head first into making the frames and stem bar, and for that I needed a large, flat, concrete area to lay out the 35-foot long plywood pattern.

There were two factory buildings on 'my' industrial site, so I visited the KBL springs factory. Machines were clattering and the phone was ringing constantly. A machine operator pointed me in the direction of the boss, Colin Barkwith, who was busy on calls.

It was a nerve-racking experience asking for some of his floor space for a couple of days, but I had noticed that half of it was not being used. To my surprise, Colin agreed and by that afternoon the keel bar started taking shape.

It was exacting work welding the three-inch by quarter-inch side frames to the bottom frame and each time I started welding, the heat would make them move out of place. I eventually worked out that, just before a frame reached the right position, if I quickly doused it with cold water, it stopped the movement just in time.

The frames were numbered from one to 11, from bow to stern, with the same spacing between each frame. These frame positions are called stations.

The frame in the diagram below would represent frame number two, so the bottom frames are quite steep and as you move further back in the boat, away from the 'pointy end', the bottom frames gradually become flatter. When they are all joined together, the stem bar, or keel bar, runs the length of the boat and fits into slots, as shown.

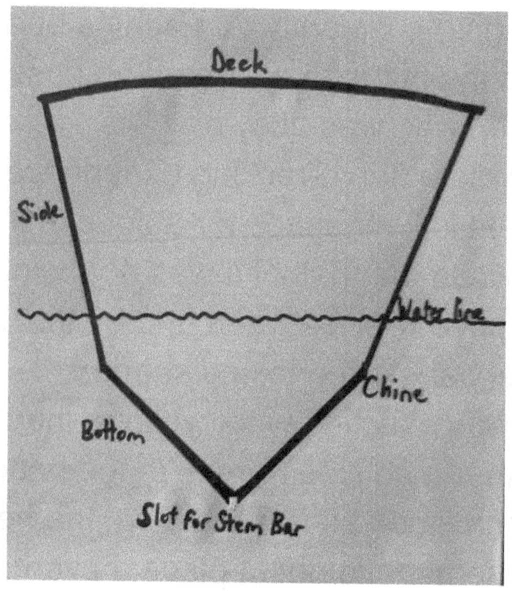

The stem bar is considerably heavier than the frames and it took a lot of effort to bend it. To achieve this, we supported it over two large blocks of wood. My younger brother Lewis held the bar on its edge while I hit the bar between the two blocks with a sledge hammer until it bent slightly. By continuing this process we eventually managed to obtain the desired curve. All of the deck beams were curved in the same manner.

From that day on, Colin Barkwith took a keen interest in the progress of the boat and became one of my greatest supporters during the 4000-hour marathon that lay ahead.

The days, weeks and months slipped by, with me driving to the boat at 8am in my little Morris Minor. (Originally I had a larger Hillman Hunter, but had to sell it to pay for winches, anchor chain and sail cloth).

The boat was now fully formed, but still an empty rusty shell. All the steel work was complete and it was time to employ a contractor to sandblast the hull inside and out. He then immediately applied several coats of paint to avoid the steel oxidising. This was quite a transformation, from a rusty hulk to a beautiful sleek boat.

Lewis put in many hours helping me with the boat and we were both learning a wide range of new skills as we went along. He would later put that knowledge to good use as he started building his own yacht.

Having a lunch break with my brother Lewis (right). Photo by J. Faulkner

I bought a four-cylinder tractor engine cheaply from a wrecker and needed to marinise it, which was quite a battle. The main task was to make a bell-housing to mount the gearbox to the motor. This had to be accurate, as the finished product would be machined by lathe to within a few thousandths of an inch.

This was one job I had no clue about and Colin spent hours, in between running his business making springs, showing me how to use a lathe and other engineering skills. Finally we produced a fully marinised engine.

Whenever I was at my lowest ebb, Colin would always sort me out, either by showing me how to do something or just talking me through things. His favourite saying was: "Patience, perseverance and a pot of grease and you can stretch a flea's bum over a 44-gallon drum."

One of the many things Colin helped with was making innerspring mattresses, tailored to fit the odd shapes required. They proved to be very comfortable. He was an amazing man who was always ready to help. I will never forget him.

There were so many other things that I needed to learn about. I had to learn how to wire the boat to a marine standard, which meant soldering all of the joints to ensure perfect connections for lights, radio, engine, depth sounder, sum log and many other applications. The boat eventually looked like a spaghetti factory, with wires running in all directions.

The same applied to the plumbing, running all the pipes from the water tanks to the galley, toilet and bathroom without any leaks. It was difficult to reach many of the narrow areas of the hull, such as under the cockpit and the pointed part of the bow, where I had to install the anchor winch through the deck.

When all of the components were installed, we could then fit the plywood linings to cover everything. In this way, it was a bit like building a wooden boat inside a steel boat.

At 5.30pm, I would race home to my flat to cook dinner and wash off the oil, dust and sweat. At 7pm I headed to the Commercial Hotel to play acoustic guitar and sing with my friend Phil.

John Yuile of the Manawatu Evening Standard *wrote an article about Phil and me.*

We played light contemporary music for mostly university students, teachers and nurses. It was an enjoyable job and a complete break from the rough physical work of building a steel boat, but I was often too tired to play as well as I would have liked.

I met many interesting people during our breaks between playing and became good friends with Nicky, who worked at the front desk. She was always keen for a chat when things were a bit quiet and was fascinated that I was building an ocean going yacht. She later came to have a look at the project.

My day ended at 11pm and I certainly slept well, especially knowing I had earned enough to pay that week's rent. It was one of the few jobs with short hours that paid enough to live on.

At times I felt completely overwhelmed and didn't know what to do. I would then go on a boatyard trip to gain inspiration by learning from both amateur and professional boat builders.

One of the things that made all the work worthwhile was getting to know so many people well and developing deeper friendships because of this shared interest.

Lyndon Smith put a lot of effort into the boat's woodwork by kindly selling sapele mahogany to me at cost price and milling it to the dimensions I required. He also made some rounded posts so that we didn't have sharp edges where one sheet of plywood met another.

I made the sails on his wife's Bernina sewing machine in their lounge. I had to scale them up from an 18-foot yacht design and used tent canvas because I couldn't afford sail cloth. I made the smallest sail first and tried it out on a friend's yacht to see how well it set. I noticed it needed to be flatter and that gave me the chance to change the shape of the other sails so they had less belly.

I was totally worn out after working six days a week on the boat, plus four nights a week playing music and decided I needed a long break.

I belonged to the Mako Sub Aqua Club and they were organising a trip to Whanarua Bay on the East Cape, just past Te Kaha. We took tents, dinghies and all our dive gear and set up on that idyllic beach with pohutukawa trees bending over the sand.

I would go for a dive in the morning, usually for crayfish or to spear some fish, then come in and sleep all afternoon and go for another dive later. I slept 14 hours a day, which shows how exhausted I was.

After a week, I came right and began sleeping my usual eight hours each night. It was a marvellous holiday, eating all types of seafood in abundance and generally just relaxing, until I was ready to get back into my busy routine.

I learned how to sew upholstery and luckily I had a friend who was an upholsterer. He gave me many pointers and was able to buy upholstery material at wholesale prices. I also sewed up a cockpit dodger.*

We painted much of the interior and varnished the mahogany trim. I made halyard winches out of scrap stainless steel because I couldn't afford to buy them. We built hatches, vents, stanchions,* handrails, rudder and tiller and fitted the motor, connected the fuel lines and gearbox controls.

On and on it went and it felt like the work would never end, but, after 19 months, *Tangaere* was at last complete.

I booked a 20-ton crane to load the 10-ton vessel onto a truck and a similar crane to lift it off in Whanganui, 60 miles away.

On the highway at 50 miles per hour. It never went that fast again! Photo by P. Faulkner

The road trip went smoothly, with my friend Brian Eames driving his ute with a wide-load sign on the front and my dinghy on the back. But, when we arrived at the wharf, there was only an ancient eight-ton crane.

A very nervous boat builder on the deck, hoping for the best. Photo by J. Faulkner

"But I booked a 20-ton crane!" Unfortunately the crane company had received a more profitable job elsewhere, so I was out of luck. What to do?

The boat couldn't be left on the truck, so, as friends and family looked on, the crane picked the yacht up and swung it very gingerly over the wharf. Two wheels of the crane lifted off the ground and the other two tyres were almost flattened. There were ominous creaks and shudders as the crane swung slowly out to the edge of the wharf.

My grandmother bravely walked up to the bow and swung a bottle of champagne. It missed, so she swung again and bubbles flew everywhere. "I name this ship *Tangaere*. May God bless her and all who sail in her!"

Suddenly my yacht was afloat on the murky waters of the Whanganui River. The Maori word *tangaere* means *to wander* in English, and it was hard to believe that this collection of metal and wood I had built was ready to live up to her name.

After stepping the mast, tensioning the rigging and checking the sails, halyards and sheets, the day finally arrived for a test sail. I motored down the river with my brothers Lewis and Tony and then out to sea.

There was a good 15-knot breeze blowing, so we put *Tangaere* through her paces. We enjoyed learning how to handle her under different points of sail.

After a few hours, we sailed back to the rock-lined entrance of the Whanganui River. A big swell was running and crashing on the rocks, so I went down to start the engine, preparing to motor up the river. Nothing happened. I tried again. Still nothing. There was no time to search for the fault in the motor, as we were on a lee shore* and approaching the rocks.

We had no choice but to sail up the river and onto the mooring. For three novice sailors, this was daunting to say the least. After sailing through the entrance with only yards separating us from the white water crashing on rocks on either side, we had a surprisingly smooth ride up the river.

How to approach the mooring was a different matter, especially as the dinghy was attached to the mooring. Despite our best efforts, and with Tony jumping into the dinghy to fend her off, *Tangaere*'s fresh paintwork received some scratches. But we decided it was a successful first day's sail and all part of the learning experience and I looked forward to many more days of sailing under less trying conditions.

This experience taught me a valuable lesson in how important it is to be able to manoeuvre the yacht under sail in tight situations. As a result, I regularly practised coming into an anchorage under sail to hone my skills, with the motor idling just in case.

Why did the motor stop when we needed it most? After a lot of investigation, we discovered an airlock in the cooling system that had caused the motor to overheat and seize. That could have been the end of the motor, but I used a steel bar as a lever, like a crank handle, to pull the motor back and forth and it eventually turned over. Getting rid of the airlock was a major problem and I had to make fittings to bleed the air from the system.

We found that we needed to add a lot more water to the cooling system, as well as antifreeze to prevent corrosion. After that the motor needed to be run for some time to gradually let out air until it ran smoothly again.

The sailing continued over the next few weeks and the various crew members became more confident. It was surprising how many of them came out sailing with me more than once. We also ventured further afield and to Nelson and Picton in the Marlborough Sounds.

Lewis, Nicky and I sailed down to Nelson and we ran out of wind near Kapiti Island late in the day. We had seen a huge whale breaching closer to the coast, so we decided to motor in that direction and then switch the motor off. We drifted in very calm sea and after a short time the whale surfaced close to the boat and seemed interested in us.

My heart was pounding, not knowing if we were in danger or not, because I had never been that close to a whale before. It took five breaths and on the last breath its tail came right up out of the water as it sounded, diving straight down. It was a spectacular sight, having that massive tail above the water, right beside the boat.

It was gone for about half an hour, no doubt feeding on the bottom. By then it was time for our dinner and, as it got dark, we had a "drift watch" overnight because it was too deep to anchor.

During the night Nicky panicked when she heard really strange sounds. She said, "There's something out there!" Of course it was the whale surfacing, making breathing noises and splashing. Then it dived, with high-pitched squeaks and rumbling sounds under the water. It's amazing how well you can hear underwater sounds through a steel hull.

The next morning, Lewis and I were eating muesli in the cockpit, when the whale suddenly surfaced within yards of the boat. It blew out putrid spume and Lewis just managed to get his breakfast under the hatch cover in time.

The whale was covered in scars, scratches and barnacles. A sparkly dark eye looked at us inquisitively. I got the feeling that the whale wanted to communicate with us and being so close to one of the world's largest mammals made my spine tingle.

The whale continued to visit us for about three hours, then eventually a breeze came up and we set off towards Nelson.

What next? We had seen most of the top of the South Island and the bottom of the North Island. I was keen to visit a foreign country, so Australia was the obvious first choice.

Frantic preparations were made: navigation practice, registration as a New Zealand vessel, certification for Category One and purchasing a life raft, flares and so on. I needed to finish making the self-steering gear and what seemed like a hundred last-minute jobs.

Chapter Two

After weeks of preparing *Tangaere* for her first ocean crossing, the crew, consisting of Lewis, Nicky Trotter, Tony Sayers and me, departed Picton. It was a relief after many days of wrangling with officials over registration, clearance by two honorary yacht inspectors, clearing customs and a big last-minute hassle with NZ Rail, who had lost our life raft. That caused a three-day delay.

We finally motored the 20 miles out of Marlborough Sounds, and, as we cleared Cape Jackson, we started to pick up a breeze. The run out was profitable because we always trailed a lure and caught three fish, so dinner was sorted.

The wind dropped early that night and we drifted for a couple of hours while watching the lights at Stephens Island and Cape Jackson, to keep an eye on our position.

We established our watches. With a crew of four, two-hour watches meant that we all had six hours off, so we were well rested. Probably the biggest danger when sailing offshore is tired crew making devastating mistakes.

We were sailing along at five knots in a 10-to-15 knot wind that had just sprung up, and "Fred", the name we gave our self-steering gear, was working well into the wind.

Photo by P. Faulkner

I was glad I had gone to the trouble of making the self-steering gear just before we left. The seas got up a bit overnight and I felt very seedy, but the next day, thankfully, the winds moderated and the seas dropped.

By the following day, the winds picked up a lot, so we had a number-two jib and a fully reefed mainsail. By this stage we had travelled about 200 miles.

By midday we had gale-force winds and we had to face into them, because we were still too close to a lee shore and didn't want to get any closer. Working with a storm jib and triple-reefed mainsail, we were only making three to four knots and sailing into ever-increasing seas.

By nightfall the wind was off the scale of our wind meter's 50-knot limit. We estimated the wind at 60 knots or more and, judging by the damage later reported in Wellington, it was a real beaut storm.

The wind was too strong to sail, so we dropped the main and lashed the helm. This technique is called "hove to", and, even with no sail up, the pressure of strong wind on the hull causes the boat to move forward slowly. As the rudder is lashed hard over to one side, the boat is propelled higher up into the wind. Then the boat stalls and the bow starts to fall off downwind, until the wind hits the side of the boat again, repeating the process.

We hoved to for three nights and this proved to be relatively comfortable in the monstrous waves. However, when the boat was side-on to the waves, there would occasionally be an almighty boom as a wave hit the side of the hull and the whole boat would shudder under a few tons of water. The cockpit would take in a lot of water, but it drained quickly, minimising the danger. This was also a good time to test how watertight the hatches and air vents were and inevitably there was the occasional dribble.

Looking out of the hatch without a mask and snorkel was a dicey business, as the salt spray off the breaking waves was driven almost horizontally. Imagine putting your head out of a car window at 60 miles per hour while it's raining hard.

When on top of a wave, our 'backyard' looked like a desert with large rolling dunes which went on forever. Then we would fall into a deep trough, surrounded by walls of dark water. It felt like we could never emerge from there, but then suddenly we would pop up to the top like a cork.

We tried to estimate the size of these waves and, using the mast as a baseline, they were around 45 feet high.

Like most cruising novices, I had dreaded facing a storm like this and I wondered if I had built this boat strong enough to survive these conditions.

There are so many parts in a boat that all need to be sturdy enough to withstand the considerable force of wind and seas. When one of those waves hit *Tangaere*'s side, making her shudder, I expected a hatch to blow out or a porthole to give way – not to mention the rigging. As the wind increased, so did the strange sounds produced by the rigging wires. The wires were tensioned like guitar strings but would play horrendous sounds as the wind increased, building up to a screeching crescendo. Despite that, *Tangaere* handled the conditions much better than I did.

It was crucial to have Tony Sayers on board with his vast sailing experience. He was second mate on the sail-training ship *Spirit of Adventure*, carrying 40 trainees plus crew.

Our only company at this stage was numerous albatrosses that were revelling in the strong wind. With wingspans over 10 feet, they cruised over the huge waves as if they were heading to a Sunday picnic.

Everything was exceedingly difficult to do because of the severe motion. None of us were able to face the task of cooking for two days, partly because we needed both hands to hold on and partly because we felt sick. When we felt hungry, we ate cold food.

A useful rule for sailing in rough conditions is "never stand if you can sit and never sit if you can lie down". I think Tony may have managed to heat up some food for us at some point, but, any time we finished doing anything, we had to lie down before we fell down.

At this stage of the trip, I did some soul searching and wondered if I really wanted to do off-shore cruising. This was supposed to be fun! Unbeknown to me, this was to be the worst storm of my sailing career.

Probably the hardest thing on a rough sea in a small boat is that we could never relax. We were continually bracing ourselves against the motion, and, even when lying down, it wasn't always possible to stay attached to the mattress. It was like lying on a bucking horse.

Finally, after four days of battling the storm, we emerged into some sunshine. It was a great relief to be no longer beating into massive seas and powerful headwinds. If you've ever come down on a rollercoaster, you'll know what it felt like trying to sleep in the front cabin during a storm.

The seas were still big, but running across them was paradise after the previous days. We enjoyed the sunshine, which also enabled us to get a sun sight with the sextant and establish our position. I was happy to see that we were 200 miles off New Plymouth, a good safety margin. Until then, we had no idea where we were, and it was pleasing that we had only drifted about 30 miles off course.

Overnight, the wind dropped and we were soon completely becalmed. We made no progress other than a couple of hours motoring to charge the batteries. It was utter bliss to lie in the sun and recover.

I did some more soul searching at this point, wondering if it was worth all this physical and psychological trauma. The answer was "yes", because it gave me huge confidence and experience for all future trips. I knew what *Tangaere* could handle.

The day passed quickly: sunbathing, washing ourselves in salt water and washing clothes and hanging them all over the boat to dry.

We eventually picked up a southeast breeze, but it died later in the day and we enjoyed a spectacular thunder storm in the distance. The southeasterly winds finally returned and we did 150 miles in 24 hours. It is good for the spirit to get along at six to seven knots for hours on end. Lewis cooked our first loaf of bread in the pressure cooker and it was delicious.

That night I got up to pee and collapsed on the floor in agony. I barely had the strength to call for help. It was the worst pain I'd ever experienced. We decided to try to get help on the radio and were finally able to talk to Awarua Radio, 700 miles away. At first they thought I would need to be helicoptered off, but we were too far offshore.

They then managed to get a doctor to advise us over the radio, so we were able to administer the necessary treatment, presuming I had kidney stones. Before long I was feeling reasonable. The next step was to try to rendezvous with a ship. I hoped that a ship's doctor would be able to tell me if I needed immediate treatment or if I could stay with the yacht.

However, this wasn't to be. A German ship, the *Columbus Victoria*, didn't have a doctor on board.

A nearby Russian vessel, the *Pulkovskiy Meridian*, only had a "technical doctor", who they said was not qualified to treat me, and language may have been a problem.

Seeing the Russian ship at night only 300 yards away from our little yacht was terrifying, and it would have been a major mission to get me on board in those rough seas.

Fortunately I started to feel better. The next day saw us running before a large sea and 20-knot wind and it felt great to be making progress again. The sun came out and thawed us out a bit, but I was still worried I might have another painful episode.

We fitted the new whisker-pole* mounting, as a bolt had broken. Tony climbed the mast, a difficult and dangerous thing to do in rough seas, but he went up like a rat up a drainpipe. He refitted the mainsail halyard, which had somehow come loose: it is essential to tie halyards to the deck when things get rough.

The wind changed to north-northwest, which meant we were on a beam reach*. We had swells running in different directions, which created a very confused sea.

Around midnight, huge squalls hit us and the wind built to gale force in no time, so we quickly dropped all sails, rigged the storm jib*, lashed the helm and went below, anticipating another big blow.

In less than an hour, the wind dropped to 20 knots, much to Nicky's disgust, as she thought she might get the night off. I don't know how much rain fell in the next two hours, but it's probably the heaviest rain I've ever seen.

Our dead-reckoning position put us approximately 130 nautical miles from Lord Howe Island and many times I thought I spotted the islands, but they turned out to be island-shaped clouds.

We started picking up Australian radio stations that day and, crikey, those "Awestruck Aliens" talked funny. But at least they played some great music. I was still not feeling well, so I started a course of penicillin, just in case.

We ran along nicely for the next couple of days and I was on night watch when a large pod of dolphins appeared. They looked spectacular outlined by the phosphorescence* in the water.

Finally we sighted Lord Howe Island and Ball's Pyramid. It was pleasing to see Lord Howe Island was in the exact position it should have been, because it meant our navigation was accurate even though we didn't have cloudless skies for our sun sights or flat seas.

Our Ebco plastic sextant worked well and the limits of accuracy are set by the bumps on the water, not the sextant, and we'd certainly had plenty of bumps.

A large pod of pilot whales visited us that afternoon. They were about 20 feet long and looked like huge dolphins.

The wind picked up in the evening, so we reefed the mainsail and left the number-one jib up for a while. We were fair flying at eight to nine knots, going fast enough to actually surf down the large waves. White water flew everywhere. It was exhilarating, but not the place to push the boat too hard.

We dropped the jib and hoisted the stay sail and still managed six knots, but with no strain on the gear. I found it hard to resist the temptation to push the boat harder and I could see why so many racing yachts have gear failure.

The following day started with a light breeze on the beam and we maintained an easy six knots. We were now well away from Middleton Reef and could sail parallel with the Australian coast up to the latitude of Brisbane, to avoid beating against the southerly current that runs down the coast.

We had another good day and it is hard to express the joy of sailing in lighter winds with a relatively calm sea and much warmer temperatures than the trans-Tasman crossing.

Lewis cooked two loaves of bread and they were devoured before they had cooled. It's amazing how life on board seems to revolve around food, but there is little to occupy the mind when things are going smoothly.

We experienced a strong northerly current of about one knot that day, which wasn't on the navigation chart. Usually the charts show the direction of currents quite accurately, but they can change.

We were 80 nautical miles offshore the next day and had another perfect sailing day with a following breeze of 14 knots. We had the number-one jib poled out one side and the mainsail out the other. The apparent wind speed was low, so it was warmer than normal.

"Apparent wind speed", when sailing downwind, is the wind speed felt on the deck minus the boat speed. If sailing downwind at five knots and the actual wind speed is 15 knots, the apparent wind speed is 10 knots.

We took turns climbing the mast to the spreaders, competing to be the first to spot Australia. At 1500 hours, Moreton Island appeared as a barely visible haze on the horizon. We were elated!

Moreton Island forms one side of Moreton Bay, a large shallow area at the entrance to the Brisbane River. Knowing what I know now, we should have hoved to and stayed the night out at sea.

It was obviously going to be dark for our approach to the northeast channel, but the area was well marked by floating buoy lights, so we decided to go in.

The first attempt ended with us drifting too far south under the influence of the strong current. We sailed out to sea and headed further north to try again. This took some hours under sail.

After much speculation as to whether we should wait until daylight, we picked up the lead light to the channel just before dawn. A little later we picked up the channel markers.

We pre-worked a compass course on each leg from light to light and things were confusing for a while as there was a mass of lights for all the different channels. It would have been nice to sail up the Brisbane River, but we had headwinds and the river flowing against us, so we continued motoring.

Several yachts were departing from the skyscrapers and city lights and it was a thrill to greet new people after 19 days at sea with just the four of us.

The first big change in wildlife was a flock of pelicans, which are huge compared to our New Zealand birds and such an odd shape.

After hours waiting at the quarantine wharf, we finally cleared with customs officials, quarantine and police.

Finally at our destination, the VDO Sumlog* showed that we had travelled 107 miles over the charted distance of 1470 miles. I think we clocked up the additional miles due to the storm with extra tacking and different currents.

While motoring up the river to find a suitable place for the night, we befriended a yacht full of

Aussies. They passed us a few ice cold cans of ale while still motoring at six knots. Paradise! We continued alongside them, discussing where to go and what to do.

They found us a mooring spot and even gave us a lift to the flat where my sisters Jean and Rae were living. It was great to catch up with them, hear all the news and have badly needed long and hot showers. We eventually headed back to the boat, which was tied up to some handy mooring piles and slept very well.

At 0600 hours, I was woken by an irate Aussie yelling, "What the hell are you doing tied up there?" I assured him we would be leaving shortly and flopped back into bed.

Twenty minutes later, I heard more yelling. What now? A couple on a balcony next door had heard the earlier commotion and asked if we'd like to use their jetty. I hastily agreed and within the hour we had moved onto our own private jetty, only 50 yards upstream.

While preparing breakfast, I heard another yell. Crikey, not again! I popped up for the third time and it was the burly guy from the first piles asking if we wanted a job. This truly was the land of opportunity and we had barely stepped ashore.

Gary and Marilyn, who owned the jetty, were extremely generous and offered the use of their downstairs area. It had everything: kitchen, bathroom, lounge and TV and we could run a power lead and water hose down to the boat. All for a mere $10 per week.

After breakfast, Lewis and I went about 50 yards downriver to work on a jetty they were building for a multimillion dollar 90-foot aluminium launch. Unfortunately it was so hot in the river basin that I couldn't continue working. I left Lewis slogging away in the heat and went in search of an air-conditioned job.

In between job interviews I went to hospital for tests to determine what had caused the pain in my abdomen during the trip. They couldn't find anything, but assumed that I must have passed a kidney stone and suggested that I needed to drink a lot more water to prevent the buildup of salts.

The ferry to the city left from a wharf nearby and when we got to know the ferry driver we could whistle him up and he would pick us up from the boat.

A few days later, I landed a job in one of the most luxurious hotels in town as a silver-service waiter. When I returned to the boat, my sister

Jean was visiting and I asked, "What does silver service mean?" She tried to explain the intricacies of it, then told me, "You won't have a show of pulling that off!"

The following evening I showed up to work as a silver-service waiter. I had raced out the day before to buy a white shirt, bow tie and cummerbund. I soon found myself way out of my depth and the all-female team saw immediately that I was floundering, took pity on me and changed my job to wine waiter.

I knew nothing about wine, but that job suited me just fine for the next six weeks and I really enjoyed the interaction with all of the interesting clientele.

Nicky was as yet unemployed but trying hard to find something. Tony left the boat a few days after our arrival in Brisbane and flew back to New Zealand to meet a boat in Picton for another Tasman crossing. A tiger for punishment!

We hoped to look around Brisbane and the surrounds for those five or six weeks before heading up the reef, exploring and diving, as far as Cairns.

I was interested in the wildlife, so we visited several different parks around Brisbane and enjoyed some of Australia's fascinating animals and birds.

We couldn't stay in Brisbane too long as there was so much to explore further north. The Great Barrier Reef is around 1200 miles long with a similar number of islands. We couldn't wait to explore that paradise.

Chapter Three

Lewis, Nicky and I, the crew of *Tangaere,* had improved our financial situations slightly, working in various jobs for eight weeks. During that time we lived aboard, using Gary and Marilyn's jetty and the downstairs area of their luxurious house in Norman Park. It was wonderful and we didn't want to leave, but the Great Barrier Reef beckoned.

When we left, Gary and Marilyn joined us on *Tangaere* just for the day and we motored two-and-a-half hours down the river to the Moreton Bay entrance. We had quite a lot of assistance from the outgoing tide and set sail as soon as we cleared the mouth of the Brisbane River.

For the first time in eight weeks we had a perfect sail up the coast to Mooloolaba. We arrived late afternoon and tied up to a mooring in a fairly congested area.

The following day I fixed the outboard I had purchased in Brisbane, and then we explored some of the surrounding countryside on the bicycles we carried on the back deck.

Early the next morning we departed Mooloolaba and made fast progress to Double Island Point. I decided not to attempt the crossing of the Wide Bay Bar in the late afternoon, as the sun was behind the channel markers and made it virtually impossible to see them.

We found a bay nearby and anchored there overnight. The next morning we motored the 10 miles to the bar entrance, which was also the entry to the Great Sandy Strait.

The sight was foreboding to say the least, with huge rows of breakers smashing in a line about 200 yards offshore. We picked up the channel markers more easily in the morning sunlight and, after much indecision on my part, we gave it a go.

With Lewis at the helm, I climbed the mast to the spreaders to guide us through the best channel. I don't think I've ever been as scared as when the fourth set of breakers picked the boat up and hurled it towards the beach at approximately 20 knots. It lasted about 10 seconds, but it seemed like half an hour. Of course we had all the hatches battened down tightly in case things went awry, but fortunately we didn't broach* and surfed another wave before reaching the calm waters of the Sandy Strait.

We learned later from locals that 12 boats had been lost crossing the bar in the past five years. I would have been even more nervous if I'd known that beforehand.

We decided to make the most of the current and carried on through the strait for several miles in shallow waters, going aground four times in all – the fourth time was the only time we couldn't back off easily and find the channel again.

After two and a half hours waiting for the tide to lift us a little, we devised a scheme of rowing the anchor out in the dinghy, dropping it and using the anchor winch to gradually pull the boat off the sand bank. I had made the anchor winch out of a Bristol Freighter aircraft starter motor, thanks to my friend Murray the aircraft engineer, so it was extremely powerful.

At the same time, we tried heeling the boat over so it drew less water. To achieve that, Nicky sat on the end of the boom, suspended over the water, holding on tight while we manoeuvred the boat back into the channel. She was such a dedicated crew member and luckily there were no sharks.

Photo by P. Faulkner

We anchored not long before dark in a bay near the channel, about halfway through the strait. That evening I spotted a lot of wildlife on Fraser Island, including many dingoes walking along the beach.

Early next morning we went ashore and checked out the bird life and I was keen to see some dingoes up close. I had heard that the dingoes on Fraser Island were starving, but some were surviving by scavenging for fish on the beach.

It is reputed to be the largest sand island in the world and forms the bottom of the Great Barrier

Reef. We did a little fishing, unsuccessfully, while waiting for the tide to turn.

After spending a couple of hours exploring a large sand island in Hervey Bay, I almost caught a shovelnose shark by hand in a shallow lagoon – an exciting sport and we later found them to be very plentiful.

We motored across Hervey Bay and entered the shallow harbour at Urangan to spend a few days exploring the surrounding areas by a car that was loaned to us by a generous fellow yachtie – a local butcher who made delicious sausages.

We probably should have stayed put as there was no wind, but, as we were anxious to get out to the coral islands, we motored the 70 miles out to Lady Elliot Island. To avoid approaching the island in the dark, I decided to anchor when we first saw the loom* of the lighthouse. It gave us an exact bearing and we were approximately 60 miles offshore in 100 feet of water.

We had a fascinating day getting to know the lighthouse keeper and his wife, who told us a lot about the history of this and many of the other islands close by. We also learned a lot about the marine life, as they were both expert shell collectors and amateur marine biologists, with an impressive display of shells. We later learned that it was one of the best shell collections in Australia.

We dived in several different areas and I saw my first turtle. Not long after that, I dived with my first blacktip reef shark. I was absolutely ecstatic as this was my first day ever diving coral reefs. It was mind boggling, with all the different types of fish, beautifully coloured anemones and coral – much brighter than anything I'd seen before.

We learned very quickly not to leave any gear ashore. In the middle of the night the wind got up from the wrong direction and we had to clamber ashore in the dark to retrieve our diving gear before we could shift the boat to a more sheltered island.

We sailed to Lady Musgrave Island at two in the morning, and, on arrival, we almost learned the hard way how not to approach a coral cove.

We approached the island sailing fast with a good breeze, saw five yachts at anchor and assumed they were anchored on the outside of the reef. They were, in fact, inside the reef and we only just managed to spot the outer reef in time to do a rapid 90-degree turn. Disaster averted – just!

This big mistake taught me to stick exactly to the navigation chart, regardless of what a situation looks like. It may seem basic, but because of the direction we approached the island from, I could have sworn that the yachts were outside the outer reef. I could see how accidents happened so easily.

We slept for a couple of hours after finding the narrow entry channel, then went for a dive to try out the "hubble bubble", a continuous diving compressor where the diver is attached to the compressor via an air hose. This allows divers to stay down for long periods of time in depths of up to 60 feet. I had spent some time putting it together in Brisbane before we left and it seemed to work rather well. We spent four days between Lady Musgrave and the Fairfax islands fishing, diving and exploring.

Me with a giant trevally

There were many varieties of tropical fish and we began learning about each one via a good book we had purchased. We ran into numerous turtles, rays, exotic looking fish and sharks – the latter were all small, fortunately. This was a pleasant introduction to the underwater life of the Great Barrier Reef.

We finally sailed to Gladstone in changeable wind conditions and secured a scarce pile mooring on the river that another yachtie let us use while he was sailing for a week.

We spent four days in Gladstone, which is a busy industrial town with a major oil refinery, power station and aluminium smelter. We decided to slip the boat on the grid* and change the gearing on the self-steering gear, by moving the trim tab further back from the main rudder. I had saved a few thousand dollars by making it myself, but it was a challenge making it sensitive enough in light winds, especially downwind.

My tent-canvas sails were performing pretty well, considering the fact that I'd scaled them up from an 18-foot yacht design.

We left after acquiring another crew member, whom we named Oz, a yellow budgie only 14 days out of the nest. He became a trusted crew member and would fly off, do a circuit, then return to my shoulder. One day he flew away and didn't return. Maybe he found a girlfriend.

It was a good day sailing, if a little nerve-racking having to sail in and out of four separate reefs, all of which were submerged at high tide.

We arrived at Heron Island, a well-known tourist and diving resort. After checking out the harbour area, which was disastrously small and shallow, we decided to anchor for the night at nearby Wistari Reef.

After a relatively calm night's sleep, I had probably the most interesting dive so far, in terms of the variety of fish life. The reserve area on Heron Island is well established in only about 20 feet of water, among some beautiful coral specimens. There were hundreds of fish, many of which were quite large, including a moray eel and a surprisingly docile leopard shark. I must have gone troppo because I grabbed its tail. The fishing was good here and we dined well that night. Lewis caught breakfast – not in the reserve, of course – and cooked it before the other lazy types arose.

We headed for North West Island, sailing along on a nice beam reach*, and only spent a few hours there before setting off again for the mainland. Island Head Creek was a 90-mile hop and reputed to be good for pig shooting. It was a sheltered bay and the forecast wasn't very promising, so it seemed a good place to anchor.

By the early hours of the next day, the seas inside the reef had built up much bigger than I would have thought possible. We were soon to learn that the wave pattern is considerably different to the open sea, making the waves stand up steeply and almost impossible to head into. We got into the heads by holding close to starboard and the rocky side of the entrance. It was a huge relief and not something I looked forward to repeating in a hurry, but we found shelter up a mangrove creek and had some badly needed sleep.

We went in search of a wild pig without success, but had a good look at the bird life and bush in the area and learned how difficult it is to negotiate mangrove swamps in a dinghy. Nicky and I had to walk nearly half a mile in deep mud, towing a grounded dinghy and receiving lots of scratches for our stupidity before reaching deep water again.

After a long sleep, we decided to take a leisurely sail up the coast to Cape Townshend, which is only about 14 miles in ideal sailing conditions. Cape Townshend wasn't recommended as a good shelter in all winds, but the wind had dropped and it was a superb little bay. It had plenty of goats and oysters, both of which we ate in large quantities.

We ate about 10-dozen oysters on the first night and I soon discovered the best method for getting oysters out of the shell was with a hammer and a stout screwdriver. That was champagne cuisine on a beer budget.

Our first attempt at obtaining some goat meat almost ended in disaster. We landed on the beach, to be greeted by five goats, but they were all too old and rank, so we left them in search of more tasty quarry. Lewis and I finally found a small herd on a ledge of a cliff, and I slid almost halfway down in my attempt to get near them. My fall was fortunately blocked by a spindly tree, but I hate to think of the consequences if that tree hadn't been there. The cliff dropped virtually straight down to the boulders on the beach below. How young and foolish we were.

However, we did manage to arrive back at the boat with plenty of goat meat, which made a delicious pot roast in the pressure cooker.

There were many turtles in the area and the following day I managed to catch five of them, purely for sport, then released them again after removing the annoying limpets attached to their shells. This was fun, because turtles are strong and could pull me easily through the water. My knees fit into conveniently placed dimples in the rear of their shells and I would hold the 'hand grips' at the front of their shells, steering them and pulling them up to the surface when I needed a breath.

These turtles were leatherbacks and they can grow to over six feet long and 2000 pounds in weight, which would be way too big to handle. I preferred medium-sized turtles around three feet long and even these were incredibly strong. I didn't think to ask what the turtles thought about being used as water sleds.

All of these attractions, and the beautiful sheltered beach, kept us there for seven days. Our next stop was South Percy Island, and after a nice sail up, apart from a little rain and fog, we dropped anchor.

There was quite a swell causing an uncomfortable rolling motion on the boat, so Nicky and I decided to take the storm jib ashore to use as a tent and sleep on the beach. After a couple of hours of light drizzle and a few dozen mosquito bites, screaming fruit bats and numerous other hardships, we decided to return to the comfort of the boat. The boat was still rolling from side to side even though we had a flopper stopper* out. Lewis had slept soundly the whole time.

We went ashore late the next morning with quite a breeze blowing and managed to flip the dinghy in the surf on the beach. Nicky disappeared under the water, holding the .303 rifle. The outboard went under too, but, after several flushes with fresh water, it amazed me by starting perfectly.

We walked for miles before being able to restock the ice box with free fresh meat. The large bags of salt ice we always bought before a trip would usually last about four days.

The next day we moved on to Middle Percy Island and spent four days exploring, swimming and socialising with other yachties. We had anchored in a calm bay in which Andy, who is a hermit type on the island, provided a hot shower using black Alkathene pipe coiled in the sun and other useful facilities. He also had a shed full of boat names. We left our name and recognised several others, including the yacht *Shiloh* from Picton, whose owner had taught me celestial navigation before we left New Zealand.

Andy was in his 40s and was well known in yachting circles for his generosity and general helpfulness towards the yachting fraternity, especially with the supply of fresh vegetables from his large garden. He was also famous for building tree huts, some of which were real works of art.

We left with two extra crew, hitchhikers who came with us on the yacht to Mackay that day, and they were able to offer us a ride in their car down the coast to Brisbane. We happily accepted because my younger brother John wasn't able to arrive from New Zealand for another week, so we filled in time sightseeing on the mainland.

After being landlubbers for a while, we sailed slowly in a light breeze to St Bees Island, only about 18 miles out from Mackay. It wasn't far into the next day when we ate some more goat meat along with a few more oysters. That was becoming our staple diet.

John had brought my .22 rifle with a scope over from New Zealand. It had a sturdy, compact case that protected it while bumping around in the dinghy. The scope made life so much easier after using a .303 with open sights. The .303 also tended to make a bit of a mess of the goats.

Later in the day we had a dive in reasonably clear conditions and speared two fish to add to the food collection, which was becoming excessive at this stage, especially without refrigeration. We would preserve as much meat as possible by soaking it in salt water and hanging it in the rigging to dry. The same process applied to flying fish that occasionally made the mistake of landing on our deck.

The next day we spent cruising up to Brampton Island, a well-established tourist resort. After lunch we went ashore to explore the place and came back with 11 coconuts. It turned out that my youngest brother John was pretty good at climbing coconut palms. We husked them on a steel pike, which was provided by Brampton Island for that purpose.

The next three days were very drizzly and misty, so we spent a lot of time indoors, mainly in the bar. Some of the entertainment was enjoyable, although tailored for a slightly older audience.

We sailed and motored to Lindeman Island, where my sisters Rae and Jean were working, and arrived at around five in the evening to a complete change of lifestyle. Every night was Saturday night there. Lewis, Nicky and I all found part-time jobs, so we ended up staying for three weeks, with little sailing apart from the occasional day sail 30 miles north to Airlie Beach.

I also got to know the pilot who did tourist flights and I found out he was keen on sailing. I would take him out sailing and he would take me flying over the Great Barrier Reef. It was fantastic seeing all the marine life from the air.

We met a lot of people during this time and learned just how a tourist resort functions. After this break from sailing, we left for Townsville, but it was a long time before we arrived. We got quite tied up in the social scene at Airlie Beach on the mainland, where a large number of cruising yachts had gathered for barbecues and parties. It was a great place to be at this time of year, just before most yachties began heading south to avoid the cyclone season.

I rowed over to the next yacht and chatted to the Belgian crew. They invited me onboard for a glass of wine and I was quite surprised how big the glass was. It had a strong and unusual flavour and they said it was made by fermenting oranges, rice and sugar. They offered me another glass, which for some reason was much easier to drink than the first. As we chatted away about sailing, life in Belgium and other interesting topics, I succumbed to a third large glass. Nicky called out "Dinner's ready", so I clambered unsteadily into the dinghy and started rowing back to *Tangaere.*

In my inebriated state, I kept rowing in circles, much to the amusement of the onlookers. It took many attempts to straighten up enough to row back for dinner and Lewis had to lift me onboard and tie up the dinghy.

The next day, despite feeling rather seedy, I decided to get the wine recipe. I bought a five-gallon, plastic, wine fermenter and all the ingredients to start production. It was cheap to make and I dished it out liberally to many unsuspecting friends and family along the way, including my sisters Jean and Rae. It was very much an acquired taste and we named that brew "rocket fuel". Little did I know that many years later I would get seriously involved in making wine from grapes, which tasted a lot better.

There was a lot of discussion among the yachties about cyclones and some were keen to get right out of the danger zone. Others suggested that it was the best time of year to be cruising, with a consistent wind, as long as you stayed within 24 hours' reach of the many sheltered anchorages. I tended to agree with the latter.

During this time, we did a lot of socialising on different yachts and didn't leave the area until mid-October. We then had three perfect sailing days with a following breeze, which took us up to Townsville via Bowen and Cape Upstart.

We could see another yacht across the bay, aiming for Cape Upstart, and it was obvious we would converge at Gloucester Passage. As we were sailing abreast, we were able to have a good chat and discovered the skipper Pete knew Townsville very well. He and his big Alsatian dog

Milo let us tie up next to his rustic wooden yacht on his mooring, which was great because the harbour was crowded.

We all went ashore for fish and chips and a beer or two and got to know Pete the Maltese Pirate, who had plenty of tales to tell.

The next morning, I came up on deck to find two large dog turds on my deck and I complained loudly to Pete the Pirate. He stuck his head through the hatch and said, "That dog took me literally. Yesterday when we were sailing towards you, I told Milo, 'You watch, we'll shit all over that boat!'"

After looking around Townsville and the nearby islands, Magnetic Island seemed to be the best and was only about five miles away. We spent a few days there at the picturesque resort with a nice quiet anchorage.

Friday night saw us ashore in the bar for possibly a little too long, encouraged by Pirate Pete and his illustrious crew. By midnight we'd had enough to drink and decided to head back to the yachts. Lewis was nowhere to be found and, after a long unproductive search, we decided to leave our dinghy on the beach for him to get home in. It wasn't long before we were all fast asleep.

When we woke up, there was still no sign of Lewis and after a lot of yelling at the nearest yacht, we managed to get a ride back to shore. Lewis was sitting on the beach all bedraggled and beaten up. After much digging into his damaged memory cells, we drew out the story: Lewis had been getting cheeky, helping himself to draught beer by leaning over the bar and pulling the lever. He also took a fancy to the barmaid. Unfortunately, the barmaid had a big, aggressive boyfriend and Lewis could only remember heading to the bathroom, then it was lights out.

But the story didn't end there. When he came to after his beating, he dragged himself down to the beach, got into our dinghy, started rowing and lost an oar, then stood up to retrieve it and tipped the dinghy over. He somehow managed to drag the dinghy back and got badly scratched by all the barnacles growing on the jetty piles.

Eventually he must have fallen asleep on the sand. We figured we may not be welcome on Magnetic Island anymore and headed south in search of long-term employment and a place to keep *Tangaere* during the cyclone season. After much indecision, I left the boat on a pile mooring in Mackay Harbour.

Nicky flew home to New Zealand and I then flew to Melbourne, chasing a girl. The romance didn't work out, but I began my short-lived career in restaurant management – at McDonald's.

Four months managing 60 staff was quite enough for me, so I quit and made my way back to Mackay in my old Corolla. It was a huge drive and I took four days to get there, including a stop overnight in Sydney with a friend.

Chapter Four

The wind was screaming at over 100 knots and waves over 30 feet were flying over Mackay Harbour's rocky breakwater and landing with a deafening crash on *Tangaere*'s deck.

This was the stuff of nightmares. At times the boat was completely hidden beneath a huge wall of white water. Then *Tangaere* would shrug off a deck full of foam like a whale emerging from the deep.

With the next gigantic wave there was a crack like a rifle firing, as one of the steel deck cleats snapped like a carrot. Those cleats were three-quarter-inch solid steel welded to half-inch steel backing plates, so you can imagine the strength of the waves.

There was now only one line on the bow and two holding the stern. Would they hold until Cyclone Kerry was over?

Tangaere was tied to steel piles, just inside the breakwater, and being close to the breakwater saved her, because it sheltered her from the huge surges that wrecked boats that were farther away.

A 100-foot timber vessel crashed against the wharf nearby. A hole was opening up and already she was lower in the water. Within a few minutes, all that could be seen was the top of the cabin. She was a total loss – well over a million dollars' worth.

An hour passed and still the wind had not let up. Two yachts broke free at the same time and a 39-foot timber boat broke away from the piles before being picked up by a wave and dropped from a great height onto the beach. It smashed like dropping a box of matches.

There were bits of boat flying in all directions, some floating and some getting washed up on the beach, while at the other end of the harbour a steel yacht was being pounded up and down on the beach. That would have been fine, except the yacht had portholes in the hull. As it rolled back and forth on the sand, there just happened to be a couple of rocks sticking up, which broke one of the portholes. The boat filled up and rolled back and forth like a washing machine.

It was absolute chaos and by the time the wind abated about two hours later, six boats were lost – four of them a total write-off – but somehow *Tangaere* survived with only superficial damage, a couple of broken deck cleats and a bit of paint scraped off. The cyclone was finally over and we breathed a sigh of relief.

Two months later, we pulled *Tangaere* out of the water to work on her for a couple of weeks at a local boatyard. She was sandblasted and repainted ready for the long journey up the reef.

In the foreground is my trusty Corolla that brought me from Melbourne to Mackay.

We had a lot of help from some locals in Mackay. One of them picked the boat up with a huge forklift and carried her to a wharf, where a crane gently lowered her into the water. All of that for only a case of beer – I thought that was a pretty good deal.

Gay Rhodes had joined us in Mackay, so we had a crew of three, and by late May we were sailing wing and wing* at six-and-a-half knots with the southeast trade winds. It's bliss sailing downwind when you're going north up the Great Barrier Reef and very difficult when you're trying to head south. Mackay was now three days behind us and Townsville was within sight.

"We've got another fish!" I yelled with delight, and pulled in the heavy trolling line astern. It was another Spanish mackerel, one of our favourites.

Me with a Spanish mackerel.

It was a big one that thrashed around in the cockpit splattering blood everywhere, before a knife put an end to that. Spanish mackerel are the most common pelagic fish in the Barrier Reef, around four feet long and delicious. We shared the melt-in-your-mouth fillets with a lucky couple whose yacht was tied up beside ours in Townsville. It was a pleasant evening, eating in the cockpit with a glass of wine.

After a hard day sailing, it is great to be able to completely relax, and the camaraderie with other yachties makes the cruising lifestyle hard to beat.

We didn't stop long in Townsville, as we had itchy feet after being on land for so long and we had a long way to go. We had a good southeast breeze with trade-wind conditions and 170-mile days were common. Thanks to a lot of help from favourable currents, we even made a 200-mile day.

After a final stock up of provisions in Cairns, we started getting into less populated waters. You know you're completely in cruise mode when you wake up at dawn, go to sleep at sundown and eat freshly caught fish nearly every day. We stopped at a number of islands north of Cairns, including Lizard Island.

Lewis and I were spear fishing along the edge of the reef when I had one of the most terrifying diving experiences of my life.

We came face to face with a 20-foot great white shark, heading straight at us. As we were quite a distance from the boat, we positioned ourselves back-to-back with our puny spear guns sticking out like toothpicks. The shark looked absolutely enormous and could easily have swallowed both of us whole. While it circled us, we very slowly made our way back towards the boat, trying not to attract its attention by splashing.

That 200 yards felt like two miles. The shark would have weighed over 4000 pounds, but fortunately for us it must have eaten well recently. Our rum slammers that night tasted especially good.

A little further up the coast we dropped anchor near a couple of prawn trawlers. I rowed over in the dinghy, curious about how they operate and needing some local knowledge about nearby islands.

We were in need of a little fresh meat, not having a freezer, and hoped to find some more pigs. They said there were no pigs on the closest island, but the next morning we decided to find out for ourselves.

We took the dinghy over just before dawn with the old .303 rifle just in case, pulled the dinghy quietly up the beach and set off through the bush. We'd only gone about 200 yards when three pigs ran across the track right in front of us, but by the time I got the rifle to my shoulder the last one had disappeared into the dense undergrowth.

The intrepid hunters set off again. Just around the next bend we came across two more pigs. This time I was ready for them and it wasn't long before we were carrying 50 pounds of pork back to the boat. Of course we took great delight in holding the pig's head up high as we went past the prawn fishermen who had told us there were no pigs.

Pork featured prominently on the menu for the next few days and pork dim sims were a favourite. The meat started to go off before we could eat it all, so reluctantly we gave the fish a big feed.

The further north we went, the closer the reef was to the coast. As the channel is a major shipping route, it gets quite crowded in places and we now had to keep careful watch for ships that steamed along at close to 20 knots. More than once we had to alter course very quickly to avoid a collision with one of those monsters.

I would like to have spent more time exploring this northern part of the reef, as it was teeming with fish and the islands had plenty of wildlife, but time was getting on. Our plan was to hit Darwin, then cross over to Indonesia and further afield if things worked out. All of the sailing could only be done in the winter, outside the cyclone season and we would have to keep moving along to achieve this.

Two weeks later, after some pretty intense navigation through miles of coral reefs, Cape York was almost in sight. I remember reading Captain Cook's account of going aground in these waters and I could now see why.

While waiting for the right tide, we anchored in an estuary just south of Cape York where they were farming pearls and we spent time in the river observing the operation. A technician who was busy seeding oysters allowed us to watch him work.

It's a fascinating procedure. He gave the oyster a muscle relaxant, which allowed him to open the shell, then, using a sterilised scalpel, he cut a strip off its mantle tissue and sliced it into smaller pieces called grafts. A tiny shell bead was inserted in the graft, which was then placed near the nucleus of the oyster.

The mother of pearl shell grows around it, covering it entirely with nacre-secreting cells, which build up to half an inch thick. This creates the surface of the pearl, which develops fully after about two years. When the pearls are finally harvested, the oysters are eaten – a fringe benefit for the pearl technicians.

After three days, the tides were finally suitable and we raced to Thursday Island at 10 knots – five knots of boat speed plus five knots of current – and quickly dropped anchor before the current took us somewhere else. We certainly didn't want to be swept onto one of the numerous reefs nearby.

Thursday Island is a very rough island with crews from dozens of fishing boats kicking up their heels and making the most of this outpost of semi-civilisation. We enjoyed a few days of ice cold beer, ice creams and movies at an outdoor theatre, which had trees growing across the screen.

One night I had a few too many rum and cokes and staggered back to the wharf where *Tangaere* was tied up beside a prawn trawler.

The tide was very low and I realised that in my condition I couldn't climb down the ladder to get to the boat. I decided to curl up and sleep on some stinky prawn nets piled up on the wharf, but as the sun came up, I felt terrible and slunk to *Tangaere* with my tail between my legs. The crew had been wondering where I was.

The following day we headed out across the Gulf of Carpentaria in the direction of Cape Wessel. There were many small islands and reefs in that area, so we had to navigate very carefully.

I was tempted to make a detour to Papua Niugini, as we could see it in the distance, but time was marching on and we had to get to Indonesia before the weather changed.

We had only gone about 10 miles when "Yahoo! A tuna!" Then another 10 miles and "Yahoo! A Spanish mackerel!" Fish was back on the menu. Incidentally, Spanish mackerel have gruesome teeth and our plastic lures were getting mangled by their powerful bites, so they would need to be replaced in Darwin. We always used stainless steel traces as those teeth would easily slice through nylon.

With a bit of help from the current and an excellent breeze, we made great progress that day. When we finally did a sun sight with the sextant, we discovered that we had overshot Cape Wessel and I decided to call into a sheltered bay and anchor overnight.

We went ashore to smoke the fish so the smell wouldn't go through the boat. Fish keeps better if smoked and another good trick was to put the smoker in the dinghy and let it drift downwind on a long line.

While they smoked, we went for a walk along the beach and came across a flock of about 50 sulphur-crested cockatoos. What a racket. I was thinking how valuable they were. To buy just one of those birds in a pet shop in New Zealand would cost a huge amount.

After a delicious meal, which did not include cockatoos, and a few hours sitting around a fire smoking fish, it didn't take much to rock us to sleep.

We had a really good run right across the Northern Territory and anchored twice in convenient bays to get a good sleep. We often saw lots of wildlife: kangaroos, wallabies, cockatoos and pelicans, but luckily no crocodiles even though they are very common in this region. We didn't catch any fish for a couple of days, though, so it was lucky we had smoked a lot to keep us going.

It was nice to be going downwind in the southeast tradewinds and making good progress. The last leg of the journey towards Darwin took us to Warruwi, which is in the Goulburn islands and also Croker Island, which is a national park. Those islands gave us good shelter.

Threading our way through the islands, we carefully negotiated the coastline round to Darwin. We knew about the huge tides, so we were being fairly cautious and waited until the tide was going in to avoid having to push against it.

We dropped anchor in the afternoon, in the big bay just outside Darwin. The tide comes in so quickly that you can't even run fast enough to keep ahead of it. It's pretty scary.

The following day, we went ashore in the morning with a fairly long painter* for the dinghy and the tide was pretty well in. I was a bit sceptical and didn't believe that the tide could actually be 35 feet. It seemed ridiculous, but I tied the dinghy to the wharf to allow it to float a long way out, and thought, "This is crazy, but I'll play their game."

Off we went into town to do the shopping, and I had to buy spare bits and pieces for the boat. Of course we also had to have a XXXX, the local brew, at the nearby pub. Drinking beer seemed to be the main occupation of the local residents.

At this stage, our crew consisted of Lewis, me, John and Gay, who were Australians. John was keen to go to Indonesia with us, but Gay didn't have a passport, so she left the boat in Darwin and I was a bit sad about that.

We finally got back to the jetty and there was the dinghy, hanging straight down, strangling itself. The bow of the dinghy was being pulled up out of the water because amazingly there wasn't enough line. Embarrassed, we eventually managed to pull the dinghy up to the steps and get back to the yacht.

The following day we were fortunate to be there for the annual Beer Can Regatta. The idea was to make a raft out of just beer cans, and there's no shortage of beer cans in Darwin.

We taped dozens of beer cans together with duct tape and then tied them all together to try and make a solid raft. The idea was to paddle across the large bay and the winner was the first raft across that didn't sink.

We didn't win and our expertly built raft, with an experienced crew and two expert boat builders, fell apart and sank. We had to walk the last 50 yards, towing what was left of our raft. Fortunately, it was very shallow.

It was chaos and of course there were people with spud guns and water pistols. Everybody was spraying everybody, which was quite pleasant because it was very hot and many more beer cans were being emptied with great enthusiasm. That was a fun day and a lot more cans of beer were drunk at the end of the race.

One of the friendly locals lent us his car and we went on a day trip to check out the desert. I was amazed to see so many enormous termite mounds, some over 12-feet high.

We came across some frilled-necked lizards, which are native to Northern Australia and Niugini, and also saw huge goannas. They range up to eight feet long and are carnivorous, so we didn't get too close.

We spent a week in Darwin doing some running repairs and getting sorted for the long journey through Indonesia. We knew there were many things we wouldn't be able to buy en route and we toured the op shops, buying lots of shirts, shorts, colourful dresses and all sorts of things that could come in handy for trading.

We bought lollipops, balloons and other treats for kids, as well as more useful gifts like pencils, rulers and notebooks, which are always in short supply on remote islands. After our big spending spree, we were at last ready to leave Australia.

Chapter Five

Photo by L. Faulkner

It's about a 350-mile hop from Darwin to Timor, and, as we were sailing along, an Australian Coast Guard plane flew over us. They had to get low enough to see the name of the boat, to check who was coming and going. Australia was clearly a bit concerned about boat people coming in from Indonesia, so they were keeping a close eye on all vessels.

We eventually arrived in Kupang, West Timor. Timor had been closed off from the rest of the world for something like 12 years and had only just opened a couple of weeks before we got there. I think we were the third yacht to arrive in 12 years, so we were pretty much treated like royalty.

I can still remember James Watang, commander-in-chief of the navy in Kupang. He gave us a driver and Jeep and said, "Take these boys wherever they want to go." We got the full treatment and were driven around to all the places of interest, as well as the finest restaurants. And yes, it was rather fun being pampered.

That lasted for about three days and we saw a large part of West Timor. I particularly remember their big banana-shaped boats with very interesting lateen sail rigs. They were mostly trading boats, often loaded almost to the gunnel with sacks of rice, flour or even timber.

It is the only place in the world where the majority of trade is still done under sail and it was very unusual for one of those boats to have a motor, so they had to be very skilful sailors.

After three days, we sailed down to Rote Island, which is just 30 miles south of Timor and anchored off the most likely looking beach. We never knew exactly where to anchor, so as long as the chart showed it was deep enough and sheltered, we just went in without a plan.

The children there had never seen a white person, as it was a very remote little island. I felt a bit like the Pied Piper, with a huge trail of children behind us as we walked along the beach. We threw lollies and balloons and the kids went nuts!

We managed to trade with the adults – a few T-shirts for some bananas and coconuts. It was lots of fun just hanging out in these little villages, where we certainly were a very big novelty.

One of the things I quite enjoyed there was lontar palm wine, which they made fresh. They fermented the sap for about two or three days until it became tangy, milky and effervescent. It wasn't highly alcoholic and, although they were Muslims, they clearly didn't mind having a little tipple now and then. It only had about four percent alcohol.

We had managed to catch a fish on the way to Rote Island, so we cooked it on the beach – much to the delight of the locals. We handed out notebooks, pencils and rubbers to the children. Very few people could speak any English at all, but they seemed to enjoy spending time with us and we used a lot of sign language during our three days there.

Lewis (left) and me cooking for an audience.

Sailing from Rote to Sumba was quite a distance, about 80 miles. We sailed close to Sawu Island, but it didn't have a very good anchorage, so we didn't stop.

We saw three local sailboats, and I was rather nervous to start with because I had heard a bit about piracy. Curiosity got the better of us, though, so we converged with the boats to have a close-up look. They were just loaded to the gunnels with all sorts of things such as timber, goats, chickens and huge numbers of people on deck. There was stuff everywhere.

These boats were about 20 yards long, carrying an average cargo load of 300 tons, and they often had only about eight inches of freeboard when heeling over. They were really pushing the limits, but it was fascinating to see them sailing up close and they were just as amazed to see us, of course.

The generic name for these boats is pinisi, which refers to the type of rig and sail configuration. A pinisi carries seven or eight sails on two masts, arranged like a gaff ketch*.

Unlike most Western rigs, the two main sails are not opened by raising the spars. Instead the sails are pulled out like curtains along the gaffs, which are fixed around the centre of the mast. These boats originated in South Sulawesi around 1906, and they have built thousands of them.

We had green sails, which was unusual, but their sails were all different colours and very ragged with lots of patches.

After anchoring in a remote bay on Sumba Island, our next journey was just a short 20-mile hop up the coast to the main town of Waingapu. It was quite difficult to deal with the officials in

Indonesia as they seemed to want to rubber stamp everything in triplicate.

We had to go to the navy, the port authorities, customs, police and often three other different organisations to satisfy their needs. Usually those offices are at opposite ends of the town, which meant we could spend half a day just clearing into a town. It was the same procedure to clear out – a huge waste of time just filling in paperwork.

When we finally left Waingapu, I decided that was the last time I was going to deal with small-town officials unnecessarily. From then on we would just anchor in some little remote bay where there was no town on the chart. We would leave one person on board *Tangaere*, and the rest of us would hop on a bus to check out the town and do our shopping quickly, then get back on the boat and shoot through. No dealing with customs or immigration or police or anybody else, thank you very much! That was a useful lesson to learn in Indonesia.

After leaving Waingapu, we sailed across to Mules Island, about 50 miles further north. This is a beautiful little island, with a sheltered anchorage and good fishing, because there were not quite as many people. It was great to stock up with fish again before leaving Mules Island early the next morning.

We headed to Rinca Island, which we had heard was the best place to see Komodo dragons. There are more of these lizards on that island than there were on Komodo Island.

There was a beautiful bay, almost enclosed by an island called Gili Dasami and you could come in from either side because it was completely calm.

We anchored close to the white sandy beach and went ashore with a can of meat, opened it and put it on the sand. We hoped it would attract a great big Komodo dragon, but after a while I started to wonder if a Komodo dragon might be more interested in eating me than a can of meat.

It was maybe a little dangerous, but we wandered further along the beach and managed to come across two Komodo dragons, both of which took off in different directions. We only got a quick glimpse, but then a little further along the beach we found one sunning itself in a little hollow. Man, it was big!

They get up to about 12-feet long and they can run fast enough to catch a deer when they're fully warmed up. They can also climb trees and swim, so they would be pretty hard to escape from.

It was great to see them in the wild. They had a spectacular red forked tongue, which they would flick continuously, tasting the air and making them extremely aware of everything that was going on around them.

Their razor-sharp claws would have been about three inches long and looked absolutely lethal. I would hate to tangle with one of them! We were very lucky because we saw about six or seven and we slept soundly that night after chasing Komodo dragons all over the place.

The next day we left Rinca Island and continued sailing east around the southern tip of Komodo Island, which is a national park. We anchored in Badjo Bay, a very sheltered anchorage on Sumbawa Island before deciding to sail at night along its north coast to Sanggar Bay.

In the early hours of the morning, we thought we were well offshore, but we then heard surf breaking too close. I did a quick turn to starboard, hard across the wind, and kept sailing in that direction for an hour. By then the sun was just starting to rise, and we realised we were far enough offshore.

That was a very close call and we realised the tide was rushing out, and all the water had to fit through the narrow channel between Sumbawa Island and Lombok. That strong current had pulled us sideways during the night and brought us much closer to land than we thought possible. It was a vital lesson about how to negotiate tides flowing through narrow channels between islands.

Mount Tambora, a huge volcano nearby, erupted violently in 1815 and was the largest eruption in recorded human history, from 10,000 years ago to the present. The explosion was apparently heard more than 2000 miles away. It is over 14,000 feet, making it one of the highest mountains in Indonesia.

After leaving Mount Tambora, we sailed on to Satonda Island. It is also a volcanic island, quite a bit older than Tambora, but the main attraction for us was a large marine national park. It was formed in 1899 by the ministry of forestry in Indonesia, and it has some stunning coral reefs.

The locals were very friendly, and we enjoyed trading T-shirts and shorts for fresh vegetables and fruit.

While we were anchored in a bay, we saw an enormous fin ripping through the water. "Man, that must be a big shark!" I climbed up the rigging and sat on the spreaders to see what it was. It was black, which was a bit unusual, as sharks are mostly grey or a lighter colour. Then there was a white one and I thought I must be seeing things.

Eventually they came closer to us and we realised they were enormous manta rays sunning themselves near the surface. When they turned, the tips of their wings came up out of the water and, of course, one side is black and the other is white. Mystery solved.

An early start the following morning saw us sailing along the rest of the north coast of Sumbawa to Lawang Island, off the tip of Lombok. We anchored later that day in Kobal Bay, just off Lombok, where the beaches were really beautiful.

We were just inside the Gili Islands, where the fishing wasn't quite as good as we would have liked because the locals did a lot of fishing.

After Kobal Bay, we moved a short distance around the coast. We had a lot of time to catch up on sleep and explore the beaches and a couple of local villages.

Sailing about 15 miles around the coast, we anchored in a bay that was a handy spot to cross the strait to Bali. We spent quite a bit of time there and just wandered around the local villages. It was quite undeveloped, compared with Bali, so we made the most of it.

I bought some hand-woven blankets and a couple of handmade knives with wooden scabbards, which I still have:

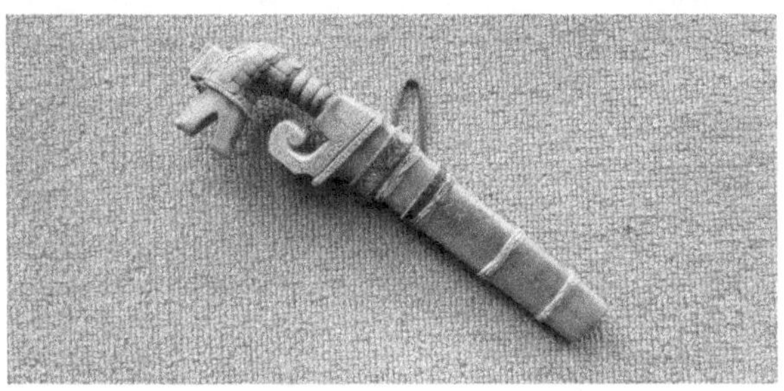

It was very pleasant having the time to just browse and the food was great. My favourite dish was gado gado, which was a combination of raw and blanched vegetables with hard-boiled eggs, boiled potato, fried tofu and lontong, topped with a spicy peanut sauce.

The locals were not pushy and didn't try to make us buy things, so we didn't feel like wallets on legs. Even though they were incredibly poor by our standards, they always seemed happy.

We had been warned about getting sick in Indonesia, but in all of the villages we ate everything that was offered and never got sick. It was fun trying all the interesting food and maybe the remoteness and low population meant there was less chance of the infamous "Bali belly".

We really enjoyed interacting with the friendly locals, and I knew nothing about Islam or the culture of Indonesia. Everything was fascinating and so different to our lives in New Zealand.

Chapter Six

Another beautiful, bluebird day with a gentle breeze of about 13 to 15 knots and we had 55 miles to get over the strait to Bali. That would be about a 10-hour trip, going at our normal speed of five or six knots, just to give an idea how long it took to go such a short distance.

We entered Benoa Harbour on the southeastern side of Bali late in the day and anchored amongst about 20 yachts. Our first job was to clear in with the usual officials, police, customs and immigration in Denpasar.

It is quite a big harbour and the boats were from all around the world. I was interested in hearing other yachties' reports about piracy and other potential issues in Indonesia, so I spoke to many of them about their experiences. Not one of them had had any problem with pirates or with corrupt officials. We had heard many stories, but

I think there was a lot of media hype, so I decided not to take any notice of that.

In Indonesia it was so cheap to eat in restaurants that we didn't bother to cook on board, unless, of course, we had freshly caught fish. I think it cost less for a full meal in a restaurant than to open one of the cans of meat we'd bought in New Zealand.

For example, in Benoa Harbour there was a little restaurant called Cassie's Place. She was a bit of a character. We usually ate nasi goreng, which is fried rice with chicken, for about 50 cents a meal. If you really lashed out and added a couple of biscuits and a cup of coffee, it cost 70 cents. That deal was pretty hard to beat, so of course we ate there almost every day.

During our many meals at Cassie's, we became friends with two Belgians – Eddie and Leif. They had a classic wooden yacht called *Kottick*. It was quite small and Eddie was very tall, which must have been tricky.

After circumnavigating the world in little *Kottick*, they returned to Belgium and bought a bigger steel yacht. Eventually they sailed it to New Zealand and settled here.

We did some exploring with Eddie and Leif and ended up at Kuta Beach, enjoyed a massage while lying on the beach, swam, drank beer and generally had a good time.

We even tried some of the local blue-meanie pancakes, which threw me into an altered state for a few hours. They're made from magic mushrooms and I remember trying to take a photo inside a surf break. Of course every photo was just a jumble of water or no waves at all, just sky – I just wasn't capable of getting any of the incredible photos that I could see in my head.

We travelled by car right around Bali and up to Ubud in the north, just to check out all the different local scenes. It was quite different from what we had become accustomed to and rather touristy. There was a lot of noise, with motorbikes and people rushing in every direction, but it was quite good for a change after being isolated for so long.

I always thought I'd like to get some carvings done because the Balinese are renowned for their wood carvings. There were a couple of mahogany posts from floor to ceiling in the boat, so I employed a young chap who sat on the floor and carved for four days. He carved all the way up the posts on three sides, and he did a really good job. I think after working hard for four days he charged about $60. That was considered an inflated tourist price, but I thought it was great value.

I still have a wooden carving he did of the name *Tangaere.* It hangs on the wall, and is a great souvenir of those good times in Bali.

We had a cruising permit valid for three months to sail through Indonesia and would have liked more, but that was the maximum time and the permit was about to expire, so we could only spend about a week in Bali before we needed to clear out and start heading east towards Singapore. I was keen to see a lot more of Indonesia and I thought the only way to do that was to visit small places, and keep well away from any town that was likely to have police or officials.

We went to Gili Selang, as we'd heard it had a great reef for diving. It was also on the northern side of Bali and was the right direction for us to take. We had a great day there, snorkelling and enjoying the colourful coral and fish.

The next day we went a few miles further along the north coast of Bali to Lovina Beach and did more swimming, snorkelling and eating up large at local restaurants.

The next leg would be 75 miles, so we headed north early in order to arrive at Sapudi Island in daylight. We anchored on the northern side of the island, as there was a southeasterly wind, went ashore to a tiny village and met a chap there who spoke English well.

He was a local school teacher and invited us in for coffee and a chat. He had three wives and this, of course, was extremely fascinating for me, because I knew nothing about wives or Islamic customs. I was amazed that as a school teacher he was able to afford to run three separate households, but he seemed to be doing well.

He loaned us his motorbike and with the three of us on board, we rode across to the other side of the island to a slightly bigger town, where we tried to do some shopping, but we were a big novelty, possibly because our crew member John had blond hair. Every time we went into a shop, people would crowd around to see what we were looking for, to the extent that we couldn't get out of the shop. It was rather claustrophobic.

In the end it got to the point where it was impossible to do anything. I remember we all climbed up onto the back of a truck to escape, and there was a sea of people all staring up at us. It was pretty weird, but they obviously found us entertaining and it gave us a taste of what it might be like to be superstars.

We returned to the village where we had anchored, after giving the little motorbike a hard workout with the three of us blokes on board.

We learned that a bull race was about to take place. This is a really big sport in Indonesia and I had never seen anything like it. They attached two bulls to a kind of chariot without wheels. It has two skids on the ground, and the jockey hangs onto a timber beam between them. He then grabs the tail of each bull and he has a stick with some tacks sticking out of the end to encourage the bulls to go faster.

The race we saw was about 200 yards long. I foolishly squatted down in the middle of the track with my video camera, and the bulls thundered past on both sides. Very scary and I don't think I could do that now, but it was really exciting.

Those bulls were clearly pampered, and probably better treated than some of the owners' wives. The bulls were often beautifully painted, with all sorts of coloured head dresses and brightly coloured ribbons on their horns.

The locals took these races seriously and they bet heavily on them. It was extremely entertaining and the whole scene was spectacular.

We had taken the guitar ashore and that evening we had a little gathering with some locals on the beach.

Photo by L. Faulkner

One of the things I remember about those times was the pungent odour of Indonesian cigarettes. They contained spices like cloves and people smoked a lot there, perhaps as a substitute for alcohol.

The wind was light, but we decided to leave Sapudi the next day. We hadn't gone far when I spotted an oil rig with a big supply tugboat anchored nearby. We decided to go over and investigate, because I had never seen an oil rig. I was looking at the whole operation through the binoculars and I saw a guy up on the bridge waving us over. We went over and he said, "Tie up to the tugboat." It was about 150 feet long and made *Tangaere* look like a little dinghy hanging off the back.

He invited us on board and we enjoyed a sumptuous lunch, with all sorts of meats, ice-cold fruit and desserts.

The skipper, a very accommodating American, invited us to stay for dinner that night, too, but he said that if the helicopter returned from Jakarta with his clearance papers, he would have to leave.

After having no refrigeration, we were suddenly in air-conditioned luxury, eating every type of food imaginable. We were really enjoying ourselves, but later in the afternoon we heard the helicopter approaching so we had to leave all that luxury behind.

As we were leaving, the captain of the tug said that since there was no wind, he might be able to tow us. But we would need to motor until we were out of sight of the oil rig, because he was officially not permitted to tow us.

The plan was to go about 10 miles and he would catch up to us. They were heading for Singapore too, so I thought it was a great idea, especially as they would only travel at about eight knots, which was perfect for us. However, when we'd gone about 10 miles, the wind got up to about 15 knots, so we started sailing and never saw the tug again.

We carried on along the north coast of Java for 155 miles, which included an overnight sail, and pulled into a small village not far from Rembang. It was another cute little village and the locals were keen to see us.

We did quite a bit of trading for coconuts, lots of vegetables and all sorts of different fruit. Rambutans were one of my favourites – absolutely delicious and a little bit like lychees.

Of course there were pawpaws, bananas and several other tropical fruits we liked.

They had quite a few nuggety little horses and suggested we go for a ride through the jungle. Off we went and Lewis disappeared at a great rate of knots through the jungle and didn't return.

We had been waiting back at the village for quite a while when he arrived at last, all scratched and bruised. The horse had taken a dislike to Lewis and dragged him under a low branch. He wasn't happy.

Photo by P. Faulkner

The following day we continued our journey towards Singapore. We got to Mankato Island, where there was a small town. We were a bit nervous about entering, as officially we weren't supposed to be stopping anywhere in Indonesia after our permit ended. But we desperately needed some supplies from the village, so we raced into town, bought everything we could possibly need and raced back to the dinghy.

A young guy came up to us and said, "The police want to see you."

Oh no… I said, "Tell them that you just missed us!" We jumped into the dinghy and took off at a great rate of knots, but we weren't chased.

It was a bit nerve-racking trying to avoid officials, but it was worth it. Instead of only three months in Indonesia we ended up there for over four months and it was great.

We now had about 350 miles to go to reach Singapore and there is a large group of islands on the way. The next stop we made was at Patong Island, a tiny, isolated island and unlikely to have any officials. Again it was really entertaining to go ashore, as the locals were more than happy to interact with us.

One of the things I noticed on a lot of these islands, especially where the jungle was close to the village, was the sound of monkeys chattering away in the trees. They were especially chatty in the evenings, making a huge racket, jumping around and entertaining us.

We did a lot of trading with the locals, of course, for their delicious fruit and vegetables.

After a day on Patong Island, we carried on up to Buddha Island, then worked our way up to the strait of Singapore. The winds got lighter and lighter the closer we got to the equator. Getting into the Doldrums was pretty slow sailing at times, but we were reluctant to motor. We didn't like the noise, the heat or the smell, and we didn't have much money to spend on diesel.

We found a tiny island where nobody lived permanently, but local fishermen spent short periods of time there. We stayed for a few nights, and it was marvellous having it all to ourselves.

They had planted lots of coconut palms, pawpaws and a number of other crops and we could just help ourselves. It was flat calm and hot, so we would lie in the water, drinking from coconuts and eating pawpaw. We lapped up the peace and quiet, as we knew that as soon as we got to Singapore it would be chaos.

That was a magical island break. Beautiful beaches, clear blue skies and lovely warm water and only 100 miles south of Singapore.

Chapter Seven

The landscape on our horizon changed dramatically as we approached Singapore. There were high-rise buildings by the score in the background and rows and rows of ships at anchor, with at least 50 miles of ships all waiting to load or unload in this huge port.

We sailed in and out of the "roads", which is the name for an area designated for ships waiting to unload. The unloading is done by lighters, a type of barge. A boat will tow four or five of these out to a ship and they are tied alongside, then the ship is unloaded and the lighters are towed back to various wharves. This system works extremely well, because many ships can be unloaded at once and Singapore is one of the busiest ports in the world.

Some of the ships were huge and we had to sail quite close to them, which meant we lost the wind behind a high wall of steel. But we did manage to eventually negotiate our way through them all into a boat harbour.

It was actually quite a big harbour, and we were able to anchor instead of paying for a marina berth. This was also convenient, because we could sail on and off the anchorage rather than having to motor in the crowded marina, but, most importantly, it cost nothing.

Tangaere *in Singapore Harbour. Photo by P. Faulkner*

We went ashore and did the usual clearance with all of the officials, which included declaring our two rifles. That was quite a performance and I needed to put them into bond at the local police station on the waterfront. I would be able to pick them up when we finally left Singapore.

The most fascinating thing about Singapore for us was Chinatown. It was a thriving, bustling part of the city where you could buy almost anything you wanted, not that we had much money.

It was fun looking at all the strange things for sale, such as whole ducks hanging up. It had a huge amount of character – the restaurants were endless and it was the first time I'd really been to what we now call a food court.

You could buy any type of meal from a huge range of little food stalls and eat them at an outside table. There might be four or five of us sitting around the table, all eating a different dish from a different stall. The food court was circular, with a huge roof over it and no walls. It was very hot, so we sat at a table near the perimeter, where there was a bit more air movement.

This was a sociable time, drinking the local ice-cold beer, which was a big treat for us, and working our way through every different type of food we could find.

There appeared to be a fusion of Chinese, Indonesian, Malaysian and Indian cuisine, including my favourite gado gado. Most of the food was delicious and inexpensive and eating was probably our main pastime.

Lewis decided to head off to the United States to chase his girlfriend Liz, who was doing her master's degree there, so I was going to be a bit short of crew. Luckily I met Karen Cruz, who was keen to sail up the coast of Malaysia, and she was a skilled sailor. John's wife, Jenny, also joined us from Australia, so we had a crew of four and were ready to leave Singapore after about two weeks.

We sailed up the Strait of Malacca to Pulau Pisang, which means Banana Island. The wind was extremely light, so we anchored there for three days because we were reluctant to motor.

When the lighthouse keepers saw us exploring the bay, they hoped we weren't walking barefoot in the jungle. In fact we did just that, because on the second day we followed a track to the lighthouse to meet the keepers. We got to know them and they told us a lot about the history of the island and the lighthouse.

They explained that there were huge pythons and all sorts of creatures in the jungle that could do us harm. We only saw chameleons, which fascinated me with the way they changed colour to blend into their environment.

Our previous jib poles on the boat had passed their use-by date and I couldn't afford to buy commercial aluminium jib poles with all the proper fittings on the end, so we made do with bamboo poles and homemade fittings, which didn't last long. Some of the bamboo growing there was over 60-feet high and five inches in diameter.

We eventually picked up a little bit of breeze and sailed all day, but only got about 15 miles along the Malaysian coast. It was stiflingly hot and the sea was flat calm, so we spent a lot of time cooling off in the water, or in the jungle, where the monkeys made a huge racket. On one beach there were a lot of white-faced gibbons, with long tails and very long legs and arms. They were extremely entertaining as they screeched and swung along at great speed like little acrobats.

After a few slow days sailing up the coast in the Doldrums, we made it to Malacca. It was originally a Portuguese settlement and has a lot of colonial history.

We planned to stay there for a couple of days, but we enjoyed it so much we ended up staying for three weeks and got to know Mr Raja, who was the engineer in charge of maintaining police boats. He arranged for us to tie up between two police boats and that made us feel very secure.

The police wharf was close to town and Mr Raja took us under his wing. He helped me do some repairs on the dinghy outboard, which was always giving us trouble, and a few other bits and pieces that needed attention.

Sometimes we would see local sailboats sailing up the river into Malacca Harbour and struggling to make headway against the current. A couple of times we helped by towing them using our motor and they were most appreciative.

We were a bit of a novelty, which resulted in a visit from the local newspaper. They were keen to do a story about *Tangaere* sailing around the world. They asked me lots of questions about my plans and eventually did an article in Chinese, which was on the front page of the local paper.

I got into the habit of walking early each morning when it was cool, and loved going around the back streets of Malacca, where all sorts of things were made. Bicycles, pots and pans, all sorts of furniture, baskets and endless different products were all handmade by these clever Malaccans. I spent a lot of time trying to learn how they were doing things, but few of them spoke English.

I think it might have been on the third or fourth day, when I was wandering around the streets, and a lady called out "Come! Come!" She invited me in for a cup of coffee and I wondered what was going on. I sat down and she gave me the newspaper with the article about my boat.

She recognised me from the photo, and her daughter, who spoke English, translated the article for me. It was reasonably accurate and the few parts that weren't quite exact were poetic license.

We got to know one of Mr Raja's Chinese friends who owned a number of businesses in the local area, including a rubber plantation and a sugar mill. He took us for a drive around the local area and showed us some of these operations. This man was obviously wealthy and proud of all of his achievements, and rightly so.

We went to dinner at Mr Raja's house a few times and were treated like royalty. It was wonderful to be able to experience a totally different type of society to what we were used to. I think being in such a small, laid-back town, and having all these wonderful people showing us around and socialising with us, was what kept us there for so long.

After three weeks, we had to reluctantly move on, and started sailing further up the Malacca Straits. The winds were light so we stopped often, finding little bays to anchor in.

There were large groups of gibbons on the beaches. I presume they were looking for shellfish. As soon as we anchored in a bay and even looked like we were going to go ashore, they would all scatter, racing up the trees and screeching at us. By the time we got to the beach, they would all be completely invisible.

We spent a few days sailing up the coast, just taking it easy. The water in that area is quite muddy, because it is very shallow and doesn't have a lot of tide flow. We didn't catch any fish, but we had bought dried fish at the markets. One of our favourite dishes was ikan bilis, tiny dried fish with rice, peanuts and chillis.

We eventually arrived at Port Klang, which is the port nearest to Kuala Lumpur. It is quite busy and well sheltered by numerous outlying islands.

We then did a trip out to Pulau Ketam, which means Crab Island. All of the houses were up on stilts, because the land was so low-lying that the whole island is actually under water at high tide.

Extensive boardwalks went from house to house, a well-developed Chinese-Malay village, with a picture theatre and shops.

These two photos show the boardwalks that went on and on.
Photos by P. Faulkner

We got to know some of the locals quite well, as we spent a couple of days there, and decided to take a group of them out sailing. That was very entertaining. They mostly spoke English, which made things easier. We managed a bit of sailing, luckily in fairly light winds, so things didn't get too chaotic. Our large deck was covered with people and, with that many on board it was lots of fun.

Photo by P. Faulkner

A few of them invited us for dinner afterwards in their homes suspended above the water. We really enjoyed the atmosphere in that village.

Kuala Lumpur was quite a change of scenery after that, with its bright lights and amazing restaurants.

We were now getting close to the Thai border and noticed a bit of tension between the Malay and Thai fishermen. We would anchor in the same bay and I learned that Malays were not allowed firearms, but the Thais were.

We thought it would be prudent, and possibly fun, to row over to a Thai fishing boat, make ourselves known and have a cup of coffee with them. The main idea was that they might not think of us as potential targets if they saw how poor we were and how friendly. It was quite enjoyable, as one of the crew members I had picked up in Port Klang spoke some Thai.

We eventually arrived in Phuket, which was a really touristy place with a beautiful beach. We met a number of other yachties who were there from all around the world.

I did a trip into Bangkok with an American yachty who knew the area well and wanted to show me all the sights. It was entertaining, to say the least, having never been to a city anything like Bangkok before.

I really enjoyed the markets and watching talented local artists at work, and I bought a charcoal drawing of a shy Burmese girl, which I still have:

I was captivated by this cute, shy Burmese girl. Charcoal drawing by unknown artist

A couple of my crew left the boat in Phuket. Karen, who had been a valuable first mate since Singapore, decided to return to work in San Francisco, and John and Jenny flew back to Australia. So I was left with a couple who had joined the boat in Port Klang, who weren't a great crew.

I enjoyed hanging out at a beach bar, sitting on coconut logs playing the guitar and singing with some locals.

Photo by J. Wells

I became quite good friends with the owner, Jang, who also played guitar, along with a strange sounding violin-type instrument. Somehow he managed to make it blend in with different musical styles. That was a relaxed, casual beach scene compared to the hectic, touristy scene there today.

One day I was sitting on a deck chair, reading my book, when a young gibbon jumped onto my lap. He was so cute and friendly and eventually curled up and went to sleep. I tried not to disturb him when I turned the pages or changed position. When he woke up however, he took a keen interest in my nipples and chest hairs and tweaked them once too often, so I eventually pushed him off.

I filled the boat up with water and supplies and got ready to head off to Sri Lanka and India with the two remaining crew. I wasn't comfortable with the two new crew members, and, one day, a couple swam out to the yacht and asked if I would like to sell *Tangaere*.

It hadn't occurred to me as I was intending to sail around the world, but the more I thought about it, the more it seemed like a good idea. At least I wouldn't have to worry about the crew for the next leg to Sri Lanka.

The potential buyers were Dario from Italy and Leslie from France. They were both excellent musicians who had made plenty of money playing classical music on the streets of Europe.

We had a lot in common and we would sit around playing music till all hours and became good friends. We agreed on a price for the yacht, and arranged to meet at a small remote village just over the Malay border.

Dario, Leslie and Jang would travel by bus and cross the border legally. I would meanwhile sail alone and cross illegally into Malaysia, because I had trouble with an immigration official. I had gone in to clear with immigration and was told that I had to prove that my crew had left Thailand.

Unfortunately, I hadn't signed Karen, John and Jenny off my crew list as required, so it was virtually impossible for me to prove they had left Thailand. The official could easily have checked with his colleagues at the airport to see that they had all flown out, but clearly he was just trying to make money out of me. The fact that he owned a Porsche suggested a lot of corruption.

He confiscated my passport and said, "You are going to have to find out before you can get your passport back, or pay a USD500 fine or go to jail." I wasn't keen on any of those options, so the only way around this corrupt official was to disappear in the middle of the night without my passport.

Chapter Eight

I raised anchor at four am and luckily the wind was from the northeast and fairly light. I was able to sail with only the headsail on a beam reach, which made it easy to handle the boat by myself as I sailed down the coast towards Malaysia.

I was about to enter a country illegally without a passport, and with no clearance out of Thailand or into Malaysia, so I was a bit nervous about the whole thing.

It was exhausting sailing alone and I anchored at a tiny uninhabited island to rest for an hour or two. I woke up 10 hours later and carried on sailing down the coast.

Dario, Leslie and Jang met me at our remote village rendezvous, as planned, and we had a wonderful musical sail along the coast to Port Klang. We all played completely different musical styles, which made it interesting.

They looked after the boat while I caught a bus to the New Zealand Embassy in Kuala Lumpur. I told the embassy staff what had happened in Thailand, and was extremely relieved when they said I had done the best thing possible by leaving. I was amazed that they thought there was no other way to get around that impossible situation with the corrupt Thai official.

They arranged for a new passport to be sent from New Zealand, but it was going to take some time. I decided the best option was to carry on sailing down the coast of Malaysia and hoped by the time we got to Malacca that my passport would be waiting for me.

On returning to Port Klang, the immigration officials naturally wanted to see my passport and I showed them the letter from the New Zealand Embassy. They were angry that I had not cleared with them before going to the embassy. After a long explanation they eventually understood my predicament. This situation again reinforced my policy of asking for forgiveness rather than permission.

Jang needed to get back to his business in Phuket, so he left us in Port Klang. Dario, Leslie and I set sail and I was kept busy showing them all the different aspects of the boat. There were many systems for them to learn and they needed to understand how everything functioned, quite apart from actually learning how to sail. For example, marine toilets are notoriously finicky, so I showed them how to replace pump washers and lubricate the rubber seals on the pump by putting cooking oil in the water.

The diesel motor sometimes needed bleeding if air got into it, which was a tricky job. The motor operated most efficiently at certain revs, so it was important to know that. They also needed to learn how to use VHF radio, with all the different frequencies that people operated on. Dario and Leslie were diligent students and furiously took notes, knowing their teacher would soon abandon them.

When we eventually arrived in Malacca, it was great to catch up with Mr Raja again. He got quite a surprise to see me back, and, fortunately for me, he had some good legal contacts to draw up a sale agreement for the boat.

I learned that there was no stamp duty on boat sales in Malacca, because virtually all the boats there were fishing boats, whereas in Singapore it would have been a completely different story. We decided to do all the legal side of the transaction in Malacca, and the financial transaction in Singapore, because banking facilities were better there.

It was great being back in Malacca again and Mr Raja generously invited all of us for a last meal together. It was impossible to adequately thank him for all of his help, but I gave him a framed photo of *Tangaere* and her crew as a memento of our friendship.

We had a slow sail with light winds as usual down the coast to Singapore. It felt completely different approaching Singapore this time, knowing that it was soon to be my last port of call on *Tangaere*.

I had a great time shopping there and bought all sorts of things. I had some suits and shirts made up by the local tailors and obviously, if you had money, there were plenty of things to spend it on in Singapore.

We met a local guy called Li, who had a recording studio, and he was keen for us to do some recording. Dario, Leslie and I played several songs together, but we couldn't work professionally in Singapore because they have very tight union rules there. Instead, we enjoyed playing casually together and doing the recording instead.

Li was lots of fun and we met many of his local friends who knew all the best restaurants to go to, and where not to go. It was a great social scene, hanging out in Singapore with Dario, Leslie, Li, his beautiful girlfriend Hayley, who took a shine to me, and our new friends.

Dario, me, Hayley and Leslie. Photo by Li

After arranging for all of my possessions to be boxed up and put on a ship, I eventually flew back to New Zealand. It had taken two-and-a-half years to get to Singapore, but only 11 hours to get home. "Nothing goes to windward like a 747."

Chapter Nine

On landing in Auckland, I had no idea what I wanted to do, or where I wanted to live. I only had a couple of friends there and they were both musicians, so we played and hung out and I eventually ended up staying in Auckland.

The Poenamo Bar on the North Shore had good live music and I met Jill there. It seems that all the best relationships start in bars with live music and we started spending a fair bit of time together.

I managed to get a job as a technical rep for a horticultural company. I had a company car, which was very convenient, and started learning my way around the big city.

After a couple of visits back to Palmerston North to visit family, I decided I definitely didn't want to live there.

I eventually bought 12 acres in Kumeu and shifted an old villa from Penrose. A friend helped me to cut the house in half, using a chainsaw underneath on the floor joists, then we used a new hand saw to cut down the floorboards. This worked so well that, when finished, it wasn't possible to tell which floorboards we had cut. It became a beautiful varnished kauri floor.

We labelled each frame in the roof so we could put it back together exactly as we had disassembled it. This worked out perfectly, with some of the nails going through the original holes.

Half the roof gone. Photo by J. Faulkner

We transported it on a huge trailer. The owner of the house-removal company was very helpful and loaned me the equipment to pull the house back into one piece to join it up. That saved a lot of money.

Jill and I were living in Auckland, then we moved out to Kumeu and got married. We took out a loan with the Post Office Savings Bank for renovating the villa and developing the land, fencing and building sheds.

Before I found the villa, I had tried to shift a bungalow from Papatoetoe, but it was condemned by the building inspectors due to borer. The owner was pretty keen to get rid of the bungalow and suggested that if I helped him dismantle it, I could have whatever materials I wanted. That was great for building a huge workshop, garage and the roof for the boat shed on our Kumeu property for almost nothing – just lots of labour.

Workshop/garage. Photo by J. Faulkner

The fact that it took a long time to do these jobs by myself during weekends and evenings gave me time to save enough money to buy timber, concrete, electrical wiring, gib board* and many other things when required, without needing to use the bank loan. So, we decided that because we had recently got married, we should go on a long honeymoon and spend the house loan on that. We set off as crew on a 48-foot fibreglass yacht owned by Fred and Cherie Peterson, who were heading for San Francisco.

Photo by P. Faulkner

Our first port of call should have been Papeete, but we noticed that the forestay was getting loose, so we headed north to Rarotonga. It was lucky we stopped, because the bobstay that supported the bowsprit was damaged. This was a crucial component to hold the mast up. Fred had a new one made up and we fitted it there. Rarotonga was very pleasant and Fred loaned us his foldup mini motorbike to travel around the island.

The next stop was French Polynesia and we particularly enjoyed Bora Bora and Huahine. Jill and I went camping on Bora Bora and pitched our tent a bit too close to the shore. In the middle of the night we were driven out by coconut crabs, which were hell bent on getting into the tent and eating everything in sight, including our toilet paper. We had to vacate and ended up sleeping in a bus shelter. It was lucky we had the motorbike.

'Hotel Bora Bora.' Photo by P. Faulkner

One of the highlights of Bora Bora was the presence of Neil Young, whose 80-foot yacht was anchored nearby. He would start his day playing some fabulous music on deck that wafted around the anchorage.

After a few weeks of exploring the outer islands with Fred and Cherie, we arrived back in Papeete. Jill and I decided that because we only had six months available, and it would take a large chunk of that to get to San Francisco, we would jump ship in Papeete.

I was keen to travel down to the Austral Islands group, about 600 miles south of Tahiti, but it was too difficult to organise a berth on a local freighter. We eventually joined the crew of the 86-foot *Anaconda II,* the largest International Offshore Rules (IOR) racing yacht in the world at that time.

Anaconda II running downwind with spinnaker up. Photo by P. Faulkner

There were 13 crew on board and the yacht was on the return leg of the first Sydney to Rio de Janeiro race. We headed back to Rarotonga at an incredible speed, 14 knots day and night, with a 5,800 square-foot spinnaker. The spinnaker pole was 36-feet long and it took five people to manoeuvre it. This was really exciting sailing and potentially quite dangerous, with huge loads on the winches and the lines holding such massive sails.

Flying fish would often take off, do a big curve and crash onto the deck, because we were going so fast. Much to the disgust of the racing crew, I would collect the flying fish, gut them, split them open and soak them in seawater. Then I would dry them on the deck, which generally took about three days. They still had a very strong fishy smell. When fried, they would be like fish-flavoured potato chips. We could eat the bones, heads and fins: the works.

When we eventually arrived in Tonga, we decided not to continue on to the boat's home port of Sydney and jumped ship again, with a large bag of flying fish and a tent. We really knew how to travel in style, especially on our honeymoon. I didn't get to where I am today by staying in five-star hotels.

Nuku'alofa was not our scene at all, so we caught a ferry up north to Neiafu and enjoyed living in our tent and eating mostly flying fish.

The local delicacy that Jill could not stop eating was keke, or deep fried donuts. She ate them in such large quantities that she started putting on weight really quickly.

We eventually bumped into Malcolm Bromalo, the skipper of a super yacht called *Netia*, at the local bar. It turned out he was looking for crew, so we duly signed up and left Tonga for Fiji.

Malcolm, Steve, Jill and me in the cockpit of Netia. *Photo courtesy of the* Fiji Times

A few days later, Malcolm said that if we wanted to sail to New Zealand, we would need to work on the boat, as large boats like that need lots of maintenance. We weren't too keen on that idea, as we were trying to have a holiday, but we finally came to an agreement that we would work one week on, one week off. That meant we could spend our time off burning through our pay packet.

We travelled the length and breadth of Viti Levu, the main island, and had a fun trip down one of the main rivers in a rubber Zodiac dinghy with Bill and Wendy, a couple from San Francisco.

We deflated the Zodiac, then caught a bus into the hills up behind Suva. At the headwaters of the Rewa River, we inflated it and all piled in to spend a few days drifting back downriver. It wasn't flowing very quickly, but we had lots of fun exploring and stayed overnight at remote villages with no road access: a great way to experience a totally different way of life.

The locals would spend a lot of time sitting around in the evening drinking kava and one night I decided to sit up late with them, drinking kava until two am, just to see what happens if you drink large quantities. When I tried to get up, my legs went all wobbly but I didn't feel intoxicated. It was more like an anaesthetic effect. Their kava had a peppery taste and looked like dishwater. Not very appealing...

I later discovered that the kava in Vanuatu is much stronger, so it pays to know a bit about the local variety before having too many social drinks.

After our river adventure, we returned to work on the yacht. Jill's job was chief cook and cleaner and mine was assistant to the engineer. The biggest job for me turned out to be completely overhauling one of the diesel generators and it was very hot work down in the engine room.

Luckily we were moored right next to the swimming pool at the South Seas Private Hotel, so I was in and out of it on a regular basis.

After two months in Fiji we headed for New Zealand. It was an easy trip on such a big boat, with every conceivable comfort. The weather on the trip down from Fiji was rather mild, which was a nice change.

We had taken on a fifth crew member, a French girl called Floride. Unfortunately for her, she didn't seem to be able to get over sea sickness. Usually people get over it within about two or three days.

In the end, as she got worse and worse, Malcolm decided that since she couldn't keep seasick tablets down, he would have to give her suppositories. He ground the pills, mixed them with butter and then froze them. Because she was so weak, she couldn't administer them herself. I was glad it was his job to administer the suppositories, not mine. It seemed to work and she came right the next day.

We had everything on board you can imagine: ice making machines, garbage-compacting machines, fancy stereos and videos, you name it. It was a bit of a luxury trip, and I think the highlight was having every type of food available. We were even able to eat ice cream 500 miles offshore.

Jill and me eating icecreams. Photo by M. Bromelo

I was starting to get used to sailing on these big yachts after our experience on a huge racing yacht and then a luxurious cruising superyacht.

We arrived in Auckland after six months working as crew, which was a very different experience to running my own boat. On my boat, I always had that sense of responsibility: I was in charge of it and had to look after it, maintain it to a high standard and deal with crew. Being crew on someone else's boat had the distinct advantage of not having to worry about all of those things. The disadvantage was that you couldn't always go where you wanted, or when.

All in all, it was a great trip, but it made me realise how much I wanted a boat of my own again.

Chapter Ten

Not long after getting back to Auckland, I auditioned for a part in a tourist and publicity movie called "Great Escapes". It was set mostly in the Bay of Islands and I got the role, not because I was handsome, but because I knew a lot about sailing. My boss wasn't impressed with me asking for more leave so soon after six months' leave without pay.

I spent a bit of time filming in Lambton Quay, Wellington, and they took some footage of me playing a guitar by a bonfire on Waikanae Beach. That was fun, especially as we used a tune I had written and got a really good guitarist to do some extra lead bits. It came out well and became the theme music for the movie.

We spent about two weeks in the Bay of Islands and it was great staying on Roberton Island, where we had a chef and everything was laid on. They had a helicopter, used all sorts of fancy filming equipment and set up 'railway lines' along the beach for the cameras to run along.

I thoroughly enjoyed the whole filming process. As soon as a cloud came over, the director yelled "Cut!" and we could do whatever we liked until the sun came out again, so we went sailing, water skiing, took a jet ski for spin or just relaxed until it was time to do a bit more filming. Needless to say, the clouds came over quite often, so we had to stay on a bit longer to get finished. Surprisingly I still had a job to come back to afterwards.

The actors didn't know how to sail, so I had to give lots of instructions. Photo by M. Fuller

A couple of months later, I was at the Auckland Boat Show, looking at all the shiny new toys available. Several people said hello to me and I didn't know any of them. I thought it was really strange until I came around the corner and there I was on a huge screen.

My face filled the whole screen, which was rather confronting. They had used the film as part of the promotion for the Boat Show, so that was a bit of a shock.

I decided I would like to build another yacht – a bigger one that would point a lot higher into the wind and go faster. Looking at many different designs, I finally settled on a Ganley Tara 39.

Dennis Ganley lived not far from where we were, in Kumeu, so I was able to pick his brains. We discussed various aspects of the design that I wanted to change. I went for a sail on a Tara 39 to see how well it sailed and spoke to a number of Ganley owners. It seemed that the Tara 39 tended to be a little under ballasted, with not enough weight in the keel, so it would heel over too easily. I wanted to increase the weight low down in the keel without drawing more than six feet in depth and I decided to widen the keel to achieve that.

This had the added benefits of making room for a much larger diesel tank in the upper section of the keel and allowing the yacht to sail higher into the wind.

Making the site for the shed.
Photo by J. Faulkner

Construction started on the boat after building a shed in the paddock close to the house. I was able to buy some temporary frames that someone had built their hull over. That sped up the process considerably, because I didn't have to start from scratch lofting up full-size frames.

Some friends helped with fitting the stem bar. Photo by J. Faulkner

Dennis said that many of my changes to the design would not work, but I went ahead regardless. I settled on a curved shape for the transom and forced the side and bottom plates to fit that curve, then I found a hollow in the ground that was roughly the right curve, put the steel plate over the hollow and drove my neighbour's tractor back and forth over it until I got the right amount of curve. My neighbour was amused by my hi-tech boat-building equipment. Whatever works, I say.

It's best to build the hull upside down, then turn it over to complete the deck and cabin top. Photo by J. Faulkner

I also added a "lolly scoop", or "sugar scoop", at the transom which meant the hull plates protruded past the transom to provide a landing platform. This increased the total length of the boat to 40 feet.

I added a door in the transom for easy access from a dinghy, which proved to be a great feature, especially when arriving at the boat loaded up with groceries.

I didn't like the boxy look of the cabin top and didn't want sharp corners of steel meeting steel, which is a bit of a rust trap. I fitted a section of pipe to the cabin edge to round it off and did the same to the underwater section of the chines*, using a larger diameter section of pipe.

These changes made a big difference to the look of the boat and most people thought it was fibreglass, rather than steel, because of all the rounded edges.

The whole process took around three-and-a-half years of part-time work. As I was a sales rep and could set my own pace, I was often able to get home from work by about two pm and start work on the boat, as I was a sales rep and could set my own pace. This was a huge bonus, rather than trying to work on the boat only at night or on weekends and trying to squeeze too many hours into the day.

The boat is jacked up high enough to pull it out of the shed. From left to right: the tractor owner Bruce, Rob (who helped a lot with my yacht and later built the same design for himself) and me with Bruce's son, my very young apprentice.

The next task was to somehow turn it up the right way without a crane. The first step was to jack up one side using timber blocks and 44-gallon drums.

When it was as high as we could lift it, we attached a long cable to the power pylon next to the shed and winched it inch by inch until it was almost vertical.

We then placed a lot of car tyres on the ground and kept winching until it toppled over. It nearly did a full somersault, but fortunately it landed up the right way.

We had just dragged the boat out of the shed on rollers, using my neighbour's tractor again.

I needed to dig a hole big enough to fit the keel into and then pushed the boat back into the shed.

The next big task was to jack the boat up high enough to fit the keel underneath it.

Many hours of welding were needed even after the hull was finished. Photos by J. Faulkner

A friend found a three-cylinder 50HP Perkins diesel engine that was out of a Massey Ferguson tractor. I was driving back from Hamilton with that heavy engine on my trailer when all of a sudden the cars in front of me stopped. I knew straight away that I wouldn't be able to stop in time, so I swerved onto the grass median strip and passed about four or five cars before I managed to stop on the grass. That was pretty scary.

Having our first child was almost as scary and I remember Jill almost pulling my hair out during the birth process. Jamie was born in September 1984 and I was absolutely amazed by the huge effect that becoming a parent had on me.

By the time Jamie was two, I remember how she sometimes liked to 'help' with the boat building. I would lift her up into the cabin so she could see what I was up to. Of course, she soon got bored with that.

Another interruption to my boat building was a loud knocking sound when our cattle bumped their horns on the hull while seeking shade under the boat.

Our son Sam was born in November 1986, so Jill had her hands full, too. She didn't have time to be involved in the whole process of building *Maxine*, but she said:

"Peter was absolutely determined with sheer stubbornness driving him at times. It was unbelievable, an unwavering commitment.

"My parents never criticised Peter's intention to take his family off to the great unknown. Instead, they showed their support and Dad, who was absolutely fascinated with the project, used to visit Peter regularly while he worked on Maxine.

"When the mast was to be stepped, my Dad provided the coin to go underneath, a tradition to ensure Maxine *safe travels. He also made a bronze falcon over the companionway, because*

the name Faulkner is derived from the German word for falconer".

Later on Jill did night classes, studying for her ham-radio license, which we would need for offshore sailing. We planned to sail overseas while the children were young, so we taught them to swim from the age of one. We were very aware of the risks involved.

From building my first yacht, I knew the best paints to use and the best fittings, and this time I was able to spend a bit more money on commercial fittings, rather than having to make everything myself.

Finally, launch day arrived and a large crane picked the boat up in the paddock, loaded it onto a boat trailer and took it to Westpark Marina in Hobsonville.

Lots of family and friends gathered to celebrate the launching of *Maxine*. I had named her after my mother and she successfully smashed a bottle of champagne over the bow.

Photo by J. Faulkner

Most of the sea trials went well in the Hauraki Gulf, with some of my family members enjoying those first outings. My Uncle Leo and Aunt Betty joined us in their yacht for one of the first trips, when we were trying the boat out in different wind conditions and testing all the fittings.

I wanted to test *Maxine's* ability to cope with a short, steep, sea, where the wind against the tide causes the waves to really stand up.

One day we were sailing in the Motutapu Channel and the boat was pitching really heavily into a short sea, hitting the waves quite hard, when all of a sudden, "bam!", the mast broke. It tumbled over the side with the rigging and sails still attached. A total shambles.

With my heart in my mouth, I started the motor and pulled backwards to ensure none of the ropes or wires got tangled around the propeller.

Gradually I was able to tow the broken mast backwards, with sails and rigging still attached, into the relatively shallow water of Islington Bay. It had a sandy beach and I hoped there weren't too many rocks on the seafloor. I attached a marker rope and float, then set about disconnecting all the rigging wires, and eventually dropped the whole lot over the side.

I came back later with Jill's brother Morgan and some heavy winching equipment. We set it up on the beach and winched the whole mast, rigging and sails onto the beach. It was a huge job and we didn't get home until three am.

Breaking the mast would have been disastrous if it had happened at sea, so I was relieved that everything was salvaged and nobody was hurt. It was frightening for all three of us on board and, in retrospect, it is amazing that my crew that day, Rex and Ruth, actually sailed offshore with me later on from Australia to New Zealand.

It was fortunate that I took out insurance on the yacht, thinking that if something was going to go wrong it was likely to go wrong in the first year. Luckily for me that was the case and the insurance company paid to replace the mast, sails and rigging.

The repairs took a few weeks as I was doing most of the work myself, with the help of a couple of riggers to fix the rigging wires. I decided to use a mast with a much larger diameter, to ensure that it didn't ever break again. It wasn't possible to determine exactly what caused the mast to break and the insurance company couldn't pinpoint the problem, which was fortunate.

Since I had built the mast myself not that long before, I was able to build the second one quite easily, using many of the components from the first.

Jill and I decided that there was no point in having an offshore yacht as well as 12 acres to look after, so we decided to sell the property. We bought a house in Mount Eden, which proved to be a good decision, as we then had a freehold house we could rent out easily.

We also had a freehold boat, which meant we could sail as long as we wanted to without any financial pressure.

It took several months to finish preparing the boat and get her up to Category One Status, which would enable us to go offshore.

Chapter Eleven

With a new yacht, a lot of systems need to be tested. The best way to do that is to go on a "shakedown cruise" to figure out what needs to be replaced or improved, so we cruised to the Bay of Islands, which was a bit of a novelty for the kids.

Tensioning the main halyard. Photo by J. Faulkner

We had set up safety nets around the boat and the kids had to be harnessed on at all times when up on deck. If it got a bit bumpy while we were sailing, we would leave them down below.

We stopped in Opua in the Bay of Islands and I was looking at all the yachts when I noticed a revenue cutter, which was the design of my first yacht. There were probably quite a few of those built in New Zealand, but this yacht had stainless steel spreaders, like the ones I made for *Tangaere*.

On closer inspection, there were a few other details that couldn't be coincidental, and, yes, it was *Tangaere*! She had sailed around the world and back to New Zealand again and was tied up only three boats away from *Maxine*.

Maxine *and* Tangaere. *Photo by P. Faulkner*

I rowed over and told the new owner, "You won't believe what I'm going to tell you: I built this yacht!" He nearly fell over the side. The only thing he knew was that she had been built in New Zealand by someone called Peter. What were the chances of us anchoring so close to each other?

We became good friends with *Tangaere*'s new owners, Joel and Letia Mendez from Mozambique, and I enjoyed hearing about some of *Tangaere*'s adventures.

When I sold *Tangaere* in Singapore, her new owners Dario and Leslie sailed her to Sri Lanka and registered her there. They then sailed to the south coast of India and along the east coast of Africa to Mozambique.

Joel and Letia bought her there, and renamed her *Solmar*. They eventually sailed to Cape Town, then across the Atlantic and worked in the Caribbean yacht charter industry for a couple of years.

They sailed through the Panama Canal and across the Pacific, and eventually ended up in New Zealand. I was pleased to see that the staysail I had made on the Bernina sewing machine had gone right around the world and was still giving good service. Later on, I did some work on her when they were in Auckland.

Meanwhile, our shakedown cruise on *Maxine* was going well. We explored the coast and went to many islands. There were very few problems to sort out on *Maxine,* so that was pleasing.

I was surprised how easily Jamie and Sam took to life on the yacht. It helped that they were so young, because they weren't too big for the tiny front cabin and they did as they were told most of the time, unlike teenagers.

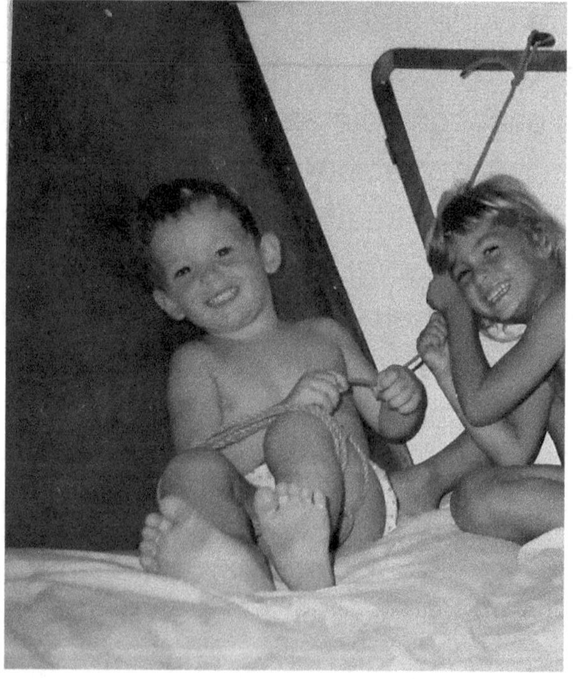

Sam must have annoyed Jamie so much that she tied him up in their cabin. He doesn't look very concerned. Photo by P. Faulkner

I made several adjustments to the self-steering gear and, as usual, the most difficult point of sail is downwind, when you don't have enough wind across the vane to steer properly. *Maxine* sailed very well on all points of the wind.

After a month travelling the East Coast, we arrived back in Auckland. It took a few months to get everything ready on the boat to go offshore, and, by the middle of May 1988, we were ready to leave.

A crew of four – my brother Lewis, John Giddens, Russell Brooking and I – set sail for Fiji, which is around 1200 miles away. (Jill and the children didn't join us as it was safer for them to fly to Fiji).

I had found that a crew of four was the ideal number to ensure that everyone gets enough rest while maintaining 24-hour watches. Each crew member would do two hours on and six hours off, around the clock. Any major sail changes or other big adjustments were done at changeover, so we had two people available.

We had fairly steady winds from the southwest for a few days and made good progress. During the previous few years, electronic navigation had developed quickly and I bought a satellite navigation system. It was incredible after previously having only a sextant to work out our position.

Because we knew our position much more accurately, we were able to get into the South Minerva Reef on the way to Fiji. It is a figure-eight shaped reef enclosing two separate lagoons about five miles long and two miles wide, at latitude 24 degrees south.

About 18 miles away, North Minerva Reef has a single lagoon about three miles wide. Both reefs are subject to a territorial dispute between Fiji and Tonga and were named after an Australian whaling ship that was wrecked there in 1829.

Both of them have entrances on the northwestern side – the opposite side to the prevailing southeasterly trade winds. A Tongan boat was also wrecked there in 1972 and 17 sailors survived for 102 days, sheltering in the wreckage of a Japanese ship.

Just before entering South Minerva Reef, we caught two large tuna, before dropping anchor in about 30 feet of crystal-clear water. The fishing inside the reef can only be described as spectacular and the water was so clear I could see about 50 yards while snorkelling.

At low tide, Minerva Reef emerges about three feet above the surface, then virtually disappears at high tide.

There was no shortage of reef sharks, so I had to be very careful when spearing a fish as they would try to take them off my spear. To prevent them from stealing my catch, I would watch the sharks carefully and, when they were facing the other way, I would spear a fish and quickly put it into the dinghy before they came back again. It was a good game of cat and mouse.

Crayfish make a clicking noise when speared, which attracts the sharks, so I had to prod a few cheeky sharks with my spear to discourage them. Tropical crayfish have spectacular patterns on their shells and are known as painted crayfish, quite different to the red spiny ones we have in New Zealand. The cold water ones taste better, but the tropical ones are pretty close.

The sharks were mainly blacktip or whitetip reef sharks, which grow to about eight feet, and they are usually as afraid of us as we are of them.

After a few days of fishing and lounging around, we headed for Fiji. We had an even better run with the southeast trade winds and arrived in Suva in very good time, a total of nine days. The entrance through the coral reef into Suva Harbour is well marked, but to make it easier we followed a ship in.

After clearing with customs and immigration, we were pleased to have some ice-cold Fiji Bitter Beer at the Royal Suva Yacht Club. It was well patronised by cruising yachties and expats from around the world, and we had some fun nights there playing guitar and singing.

We spent a couple of days in Suva, then Lewis and Russell flew home and Jill flew up with the kids. John Giddens stayed on to do some cruising with us. We made the most of all the facilities in Suva, like movie theatres, restaurants and the yacht club, as well as stocking up on provisions. There was quite a lot more rain than we wanted, hence the name "Soggy Suva", so we didn't stay there long.

We were always on the lookout for other yachts with kids on board so Jamie and Sam would have friends to play with. We came across a yacht called *Cool Change* from Chicago, with Gary, Karen and their two kids, Sharon and Brian, on board.

We decided to team up with them for a trip down to Kandavu, which is a very big island directly south of Suva. We spent several days exploring the various bays and had great diving there. The water was really clear, so we were able to spear a few fish, hang out with the locals and just generally relax.

Sam and me with Gary. Photo by J. Faulkner

We then did an overnight passage of 120 miles from Kandavu to the Lau Group.

I was alone on watch, and, just as it was getting light, Boomf!! The boat shuddered and almost stopped. I was thrown forward against the cabin top and a massive whale's tail whacked on the water right next to the cockpit. The water turned red with what I assumed was blood and I thought I had injured the poor whale while it was innocently sleeping on the surface.

I learned later that when they get a fright they disgorge a vast quantity of reddish-brown liquid as a sort of protection mechanism. The whale was about 60 feet long and I must have hit it at an angle, otherwise a 30-ton whale would have stopped 10-ton *Maxine* in her tracks.

We anchored at an island called Vanua Balavu and, as I was concerned about underwater damage from the whale collision, I dived to inspect the hull. All I found were a few scratches from barnacles on the whale's back.

It had come very close to wiping out our depth-sounder transducer, but luckily no major damage was done. We might not have got off so lightly if we had been in a wooden boat. Hopefully the whale recovered.

The Lau Group is quite a long way offshore, with 60 islands stretching down towards Tonga. One of the main attractions for us was that there were few tourists.

Vanua Balavu had a beautiful abandoned stone house with an orchard. I'm not sure what its history is, but they had planted many soursop trees and we absolutely adored soursop. Some of the fruit were as big as footballs and absolutely delicious and super sweet, like a cross between a pineapple and a banana, with a fizzy tang. They are in the same family as the custard apple. We would put some in the fridge and chill them down like ice cream. It was hard to stop eating them.

We were still hanging out with *Cool Change* and we had also met a retired American doctor, Don Miller, and his wife Mary Lou, from Indiana, on their yacht *Horizon*. We kept a visitors' book on *Maxine* and Don and Mary Lou wrote the following:

"From shark curry to delicious pressure cooker banana bread. Thank you for your hospitality!"

It was fabulous snorkelling in the large lagoon surrounded by coral, and we had plenty of fish to choose from. We ended up spending a week there altogether and would help the locals put down a lovo, which is an oven in the ground.

One time, my job was to make up cassava and coconut balls, which are sticky and sweet, then wrap them in pieces of banana leaf, tie them up and put them in the lovo with fish, pork, taro and various greens.

Making cassava balls for the lovo. Photo by J. Faulkner

I think one of my favourite vegetable dishes was palusami, which is taro leaves with their stems removed and cooked three times to get rid of the harsh tasting compounds in the leaves. Mixed with coconut cream, they are absolutely delicious.

We could easily have spent longer in this island group, but Fiji has over 300 islands to explore, so we decided to move on.

We headed to Levuka, which is the old capital of Fiji. It was a small, friendly and quaint town, with colonial facades on the shops along the waterfront. We enjoyed a few days there, shopping, eating ice creams and, of course, drinking the occasional beer.

We then headed out to another island called Makogai, where they had set up turtle breeding areas and brought in eggs from the wild. They had large tanks, where they tried to grow the turtles big enough to survive in the wild. Jamie and Sam loved watching those little baby turtles!

They would bring in mature clams, up to two feet across, and take eggs from the females or sperm from the males. We watched the scientists checking eggs under a microscope to see if they had been fertilised. They grew in aerated tanks until they reached two inches, when they were put into cages on the seabed to grow without any danger from predators.

I got to know the staff and volunteered to dive on the cages to clean off algae. The cages were in 20 feet of water and the research centre provided scuba gear. When I disturbed the algae, it attracted many beautiful tropical fish, so that made the job fun.

When the clams were over three inches in diameter, they were spread over various reefs to repopulate the whole area. The locals were keen to eat giant clams and turtles, but I believe that has now been banned.

Another project that the government set up on the island was raising tropical Barbados Black Belly sheep. They have hair like a goat, so are better suited to the warm weather. We would hike over to the other side of the island to see them and en route we noticed a derelict hospital, which was originally a leper colony.

From Makogai, we sailed 55 miles north to Savusavu, on the second largest island in Fiji, Vanua Levu. It was quite a thriving settlement with good anchorages for yachts.

We explored quite a few bays and little islands and caught two large Spanish mackerel, featured in this photo of Jill, Jamie, Sam and me. This became our Christmas card that year and is still one of my favourite photos:

Chapter Twelve

Heading to windward in Fiji. Photo by S. Tobin

We left the sleepy little town of Savusavu and the convenience of the yacht club and headed around the northern side of Viti Levu. It is completely surrounded by a coral reef and the navigation markers aren't always maintained properly. So, we were very cautious as we sailed through the channel between the mainland and the reef. This should only be done between the hours of ten am and two pm, when the sun is high enough to clearly see the reef. If the sun is too low, it causes reflections on the surface, making it exceedingly difficult to see underwater.

Someone had to sit on the spreaders, wearing polarised glasses, to get a better view of the channel. The steps on the mast up to the first spreaders made that easier. We had a couple of close calls with channel markers missing, or facing the wrong way, which could have been disastrous.

It took three days sailing to reach the western side of Viti Levu, always with two fishing lines trailing behind us. We eventually headed to Lautoka to buy provisions. It is a major centre for sugarcane processing and the sugar plant has a distinctive, pleasant smell. They also made Bounty rum there, which I had to sample. We loved chewing sugarcane stems and, unlike refined sugar, they don't rot your teeth.

There was a great fresh fruit and vegetable market and it was a wonderful luxury having a fridge and freezer on *Maxine* to keep them fresh. We would run the motor for one hour each day to chill the fridge and freezer.

Lautoka also had an excellent restaurant called the Snax Bar, which served delicious Indian vegetarian food. I think my favourite was the masala dosa. Jamie and Sam's favourite treat there was mango lassi, a yoghurt and mango smoothie. There was a supermarket nearby and a picture theatre, so we had plenty of entertainment.

We were also able to come alongside the wharf and fill the boat up with fresh water and diesel. The diesel tank only needed filling about once a year, because we mostly sailed.

The western side of Fiji gets most of the tourists, with many resorts to choose from, and we chose Musket Cove, about 15 miles to the south.

Musket Cove is well set up for yachties, unlike most resorts. The owners, Dick and Carol Smith, had installed numerous moorings for yachts to tie up to and catered for all our needs. They even had a one dollar bar for yachties, separate from the rest of the resort. Every evening, many of us would gather there to socialise, right on the beach, looking out over the yachts. Dick and Carol also developed Plantation Island and Beachcomber Island resorts.

Jamie and Sam were keen on the swimming pool at Musket Cove and it was quite difficult to get them out at times. With so many other yachts there, they had plenty of kids to play with.

It wasn't far to the outer reef, but inside the main reef was calm and perfect for snorkelling and diving among the smaller reefs. I didn't spear any fish because it is a sought-after tourist destination, where small boatloads of tourists would come to snorkel among all the beautiful fish.

There were spectacular huge cod, in particular the potato cod, which can get up to six-feet long and 200 pounds. They have huge mouths, which are extra impressive when viewed up close with a dive mask, as it magnifies everything underwater. They looked like they could swallow us whole.

A number of reef sharks were so well known at the resort that they had names. I remember one was called George and he and his friend had decided they owned that territory. Some people would feed them, which I didn't think was a very good idea, but anything to keep the tourists happy.

After a hard day's snorkelling, we would return to our mooring at Musket Cove and head to the one dollar bar to catch up with some of our yachting friends. Bob McKeane, aka Bobby Bunter as the kids called him, became a good friend.

Bob, Jamie and me in my fancy pants. Photo by J. Faulkner

He and his girlfriend Wendy had sailed his yacht *Callisto* from Sydney. He used to play drums in an Australian band, so we also called him "Bongo Bob". He drew a picture in our visitors' book, depicting the five yachts that stayed through the cyclone season. In the picture, you can see the one dollar bar, with Jill trying to drag Sam off the roof, Jamie's friends Budgie and Carli up a palm tree and our musical trio playing:

Drawing by Bob McKeane

We also met Dave and Mary on a yacht called *Vivant* from California. Dave was formerly a nuclear submarine engineer and had spent over eight years of his life underwater. Nuclear subs can stay submerged for at least three months at a time. While working on the submarines, he couldn't drink alcohol, so he made up for lost time at the one dollar bar. Mary was a good flute player, so Bob, Mary and I would often get together for a music jam.

Dave and Mary on Vivant. *Photo by P. Faulkner*

A more family oriented resort on Malolo Lailai Island is Plantation Resort, which had some entertainment that Jamie and Sam really enjoyed. The children also liked swimming in a different pool and it gave us a change of scenery. We hung out there for a couple of weeks and then decided to head north to Malolo Island for a night to check out the entertainment.

The next stop was Mana Island, which is a big resort and Bob and his crew came along with us. Bob was a real entrepreneur and he arranged for us to play some music in the main lounge at Mana in return for free drinks, meals and a bungalow for a few nights. That suited us just fine and it was great staying there for a few days. Jamie and Sam made great use of the pool and had fun with some new playmates.

During those idyllic moments in the islands, I would sometimes wonder if I was lazing my life away. I was used to being extremely busy and working hard, so it took some time to adjust to a slower pace of life. I gradually adapted and there was always something to fill in the day, like boat maintenance, baking bread, brewing beer or other such important jobs.

On a calm day, while anchored with the other yachts at Mana, I went to visit Bob. While we chatted, I could see two-year-old Sam over on *Maxine*, strolling along the deck, tapping the rail with his hand. *Maxine* rolled gently just as Sam reached the open gate in the railing and he fell overboard.

Luckily, Jill always made sure he wore his life jacket, so he floated. John Giddens hit the water about one second after Sam fell and I followed a couple of seconds later. Sam was fine after coughing up salt water and getting over his fright. But boy was I in trouble for leaving the side gate open!

Sam and Jamie enjoying the warm shallows. Photo by P. Faulkner

We decided it was time to do a trip up the Yasawas, a long string of islands running north to south. Those islands were much more remote and we were usually able to find an anchorage with only a tiny village nearby.

We always had a supply of kava on board to take to the village chief. Kava is quite expensive and takes a long time to grow, so, even though they grew their own, it was always appreciated. The kava was always presented to the chief in a traditional ceremony and was usually followed by singing. Their harmonies were so beautiful they gave me goosebumps. If we were there on a Sunday, the locals would invite us to church. We always accepted, because the best singers in the village would be harmonising and the sound was enhanced by the churches' great acoustics.

After church there was usually a delicious lunch at one of the houses, where they laid the feast out on a long bolt of cloth down the centre of the room. We would sit on grass mats to enjoy the feast, including some of my favourites: palusami, kokoda and cassava.

Alcohol was forbidden in the villages, so I would drink my home brew beer on the boat. I always had beer kits on board, so I could have a constant supply of cheap beer.

Their houses were basic, consisting of one or two rooms, with no bathroom or kitchen. Cooking was done in a separate cook house, while on special occasions they cooked outside in a lovo.

When someone killed a pig, cow or goat, the meat couldn't be stored. If there was too much, they would share the meat with other villages so it would be eaten quickly.

The villagers were really hospitable and loved Jamie and Sam. They called Sam *Samulailai*, which means 'little Sam'.

They always had big gardens, so we traded T-shirts and other things we had brought along to trade for fresh produce, such as bananas, coconuts, cassava and various greens. It was a nice change from resort life and the snorkelling was great.

Blue Lagoon cruise boats would come through the Yasawas, so occasionally we would be inundated with tourists, but fortunately we could just move to the next island.

After a couple of weeks island hopping in the Yasawas, we sailed back to Lautoka to stock up on water and food, then headed to Denarau, which has a large marina with some big hotels. The Regent Hotel put on shows, so we would buy a drink and sip it slowly while enjoying the entertainment.

Denarau had a bus service to Nadi and we all enjoyed our 'tour' in the open-sided bus. Nadi was not an attractive city, but it had good movie theatres and a wider choice of shops, so we could stock up well for our next adventure.

The hardware shops were well stocked for the locals, so on one occasion I even managed to buy a sheet of plywood and timber. It was quite a challenge getting it all onto the bus, not to mention getting it into the dinghy. Back in

Denarau we mingled with the other guests at the flash hotel pools and bars and pretended we belonged there.

We returned to Musket Cove, which had a good workshop and I used the plywood to build a permanent cover for the cockpit. I was so glad I did that, because it was great to get shelter from the hot sun.

Wendy, Jamie, Sam and my mother Maxine, who had dropped in on her way back from the United States. Photo by P. Faulkner

Dick and Carol Smith invited us to cocktail hour at their house, which was way up the hill above the resort. It was great having gatherings like that to meet a lot of other yachties and some of the management from Musket Cove resort.

We also caught up with Radio Fred, an avid ham-radio operator who lived just below Dick and Carol's house. Fred was the accountant for Musket Cove, an eccentric English chap who did not like wearing clothes. His skin was leathery, like a lizard who'd been basking in the sun too long.

He would ride his quad bike down the hill, stark naked and smoking a big cigar, to do the resort's books. He was always up early, fortunately for the guests. He did occasionally wear speedos. Fred was a real character and, after we left Fiji, we would chat to him regularly on our ham radio.

The kids enjoyed being back into their swimming pool routine while we adults socialised and went fishing and snorkelling.

This carried on for about six months, when we had to decide whether we should stay in Fiji for the cyclone season or head back to New Zealand to wait for it to end.

As I was keen to carry on further west towards Australia, I was reluctant to go south as far as New Zealand and sail back up again the following year, so we decided to spend the cyclone season in Fiji.

It pays to be careful about these decisions, as cyclones can be devastating, with winds of 150 miles an hour. I would only have considered it if there was a really good cyclone shelter nearby and luckily the Lautoka River was one of the most sheltered places in Western Fiji.

With the other four yachts, we formed the 'Fiji Anticyclone Club' and set about having fun, as usual.

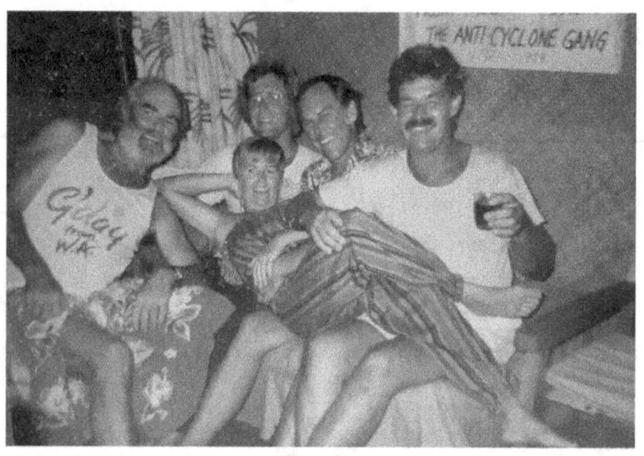

Bob, Mary and I with friends. Photo by J. Faulkner

I would often go out spear fishing with Dave off his yacht *Vivant*. He was an avid spear fisherman and keen to spear a good-sized giant trevally. They are extremely fast, which makes them quite a challenge to spear, but we kept at it until we got a couple, along with a variety of other fish, including coral trout. We even speared a Spanish mackerel. They are also extremely fast and usually we couldn't get close enough to have a shot at them.

We also had plenty of time to get together with Bongo Bob again and Mary on flute, jamming around the bonfire at night, and Jamie and Sam had Budgie and Carli to entertain them:

Budgie and Carli don't look like they're having much fun!
Photo by J. Faulkner

Jill and I would take turns having all four kids on our boat, then their parents, Ed and Juana Lovell, would have all four on their boat *Phalarope* to give us a break. Ed was a keen surfer, and was often away for hours searching for the perfect wave.

After we left Fiji, we planned to meet up with them in Queensland, but Ed became Professor of Marine Biology at the University of Suva, so they ended up staying in Fiji. He also did some consulting on reef health in other South Pacific countries. However, we've managed to keep in touch for almost 40 years.

Ed, Juana, Budgie and Carli on Phlarope. Photo by P. Faulkner

We did many trips up the Yasawas and to different resorts, such as Beachcomber and Mana. If I struggled to repair something, our friend Dave the engineer was always keen to help. We kept a careful eye on cyclones forming north of Fiji, because they form in the warmer waters around the tropics, then spin off in various directions.

That season 13 cyclones formed north of Fiji and three of them came straight at the Fiji islands, so we were watching them closely. Luckily two veered off somewhere else, but one kept coming and looked like it was going to be a direct hit.

We all raced up the Lautoka River, dropped anchor and tied lines in every direction to the huge mangroves. It looked like a huge spider's web.

That spot was considered one of the safest places because the mangroves were so thick and didn't allow much debris and logs to come flying down the river from the flooding caused by heavy rain upstream. One of the most dangerous things is a big log taking out the anchor line, letting the boat drift free.

Luckily for us, the cyclone did most of its damage along the edge of the Yasawas. The wind rose to about 70 knots at its peak where we were sheltering and it was screeching in the rigging, but we were pretty comfortable down at water level. The big mangroves protected us well, but it rained solidly for three days and three nights.

I had never seen rain as heavy as that. We were forever pulling the dinghy in to drain the water out.

During the cyclone, Jamie and Sam were shipped off to *Phalarope* next door with their two friends and it was bliss having peace and quiet for a day. The following day we had all four of them on board *Maxine*. It was chaotic but very entertaining for Jamie and Sam.

The spring on the yacht's starter motor broke, so naturally I chose that day to go into Lautoka to buy a spring. The rain was torrential. John and I put on our raincoats and bailed the dinghy enough to float. We had to keep bailing it out constantly during our trip to town.

We found the right spring for the starter motor, because one good thing about Perkins engines is that they're used on tractors and there are plenty of spare parts available in Fiji because of all the farming, especially sugarcane. It was also cheap, unlike most marine engine parts and, most importantly, it worked.

Kids' birthday parties were a big feature of our time in Fiji, with so many families around. They would become quite an event, with piñatas to break open and all sorts of games. The staff at Musket Cove were a big help, as we'd got to know them well by then and they couldn't do enough for us when we were trying to organise a party.

There were a number of charter boats operating out of Musket Cove and Plantation Island resorts. One of them was *La Violante*, which was a big, old, sailing boat. She was originally a leeboard* ketch, built in Holland in 1922 for transporting cargo on European rivers. She then became a charter boat in the Caribbean, before coming to Fiji to take tourists out for week-long trips.

Other yachties were often curious as to why I hardly did any work on my boat and I said 'because I built her properly in the first place and she was new'. Inevitably, though, there were a few little maintenance jobs on the refrigeration system or the motor.

We had really settled into our Fijian lifestyle and, before we knew it, a year had gone by. We enjoyed living on board as a family of five, including our friend John Gidden, who was great with the children and helpful in every way.

The Fijian immigration department was kind and allowed us to extend our three-month visa three times.

Since we were enjoying cruising life so much, we started to plan a new adventure westward, to Vanuatu.

Chapter Thirteen

The time had finally come to leave Fiji, after a wonderful year hanging out with a lot of friends, diving and spending time in the villages.

We set off first thing in the morning on 17 May 1989 and, just as we were about to go through the pass in the reef, the *Bounty* sailed in from Australia. It was quite a sight and we got a photo sailing alongside the square-rigged sailing ship that was built in Nova Scotia in 1960.

The old and the new. Photo by P. Faulkner

We left through the gap in the reef and came up against a very fickle wind. It kept changing direction and there were a few rain squalls coming through, which made for very frustrating sailing. John and I were continually reefing the main and the jib, only to find that two hours later the wind would change and we'd have to raise the sails again. It went on and on and the sea was quite choppy.

It was Jamie and Sam's first ocean crossing and poor Jamie got really seasick. She was already pretty skinny and, by the time we got to Vanuatu four days later, she was not a happy chappy. But she soon came right after putting her feet on terra firma on Erromango Island.

We spent a couple of days in a village and it was amazing how much more primitive village life was there than in Fiji. They lived in mud huts with thatched roofs and nobody spoke English, apart from one young chap who was doing a survey for the government. I can't remember what the survey was about, but we were lucky he was able to translate for us.

There were pigs and chickens running around and Sam was given a chicken to carry. He decided it was his and, when it was time to return to the boat that night, there was no way he was giving up his chicken. It had to be prised off him.

Sam tightly clutching 'his' chicken. Photo by P. Faulkner

We spent three days there and did some snorkelling, but mostly just hung out in the village and learned a lot about life in Vanuatu.

I'd always wanted to see the vine jumping, which is a rite of passage for young men, so one of the locals directed us to the best place.

It was spectacular and they jumped from a much greater height than I expected. Apparently the g-forces experienced in vine jumping are the highest of any natural activity. Jet fighter pilots would be the only humans experiencing higher g-forces than this and they have special equipment to prevent them from blacking out.

We then headed to the main island, Efate, where we were able to stock up at the local markets and go to the supermarket.

There was malaria in Vanuatu, so we were very cautious, anchoring well offshore and shutting the boat down at night to ensure we didn't let any mosquitoes in. We decided not to stay very long, mainly because we didn't want the kids to take malaria drugs and we certainly didn't want to get a dose of malaria ourselves.

At Port Vila, a big game-fishing boat was tied up alongside the wharf, and they had a massive marlin, which was well over 600 pounds. It was amazing to see it up close.

Sam and Jamie with the marlin. Photo by P. Faulkner

After a couple of days in Vila, stocking up and checking out the city, we again set sail. Our fishing lines trailed behind us as always and this time we hooked a marlin. That was not our intention at all and the huge fish 'tail walked' behind the boat!

There was no way we could have landed a huge marlin on our yacht, especially with all our gear in the way. The cockpit was full of things and the self-steering gear was in the way, so we didn't want a marlin thrashing around in there. Fortunately, it eventually straightened the twin high-tensile stainless steel hooks and escaped.

We decided to visit the Huon Island reef complex, which is about 100 miles north of the northern tip of New Caledonia. It was en route to Gladstone, Australia, and I wanted to avoid going into a port and dealing with officials for such a short stay.

There are four sand cays scattered around the reef: Huon, Le Leizour, Fabre and Surprise. Each island is about half a mile across and the total land area is about 160 acres. They rise only 10 feet above the water at high tide, so they're not much more than a sand bank with occasional scrubby plants. At one stage, the islands were mined for guano, because of the huge amount of birdlife there.

It was convenient to have a GPS to take us right to the edge of the reef without too much danger and there was an automated lighthouse. The reef was v-shaped and very open to the north, so we sailed around the edge of the reef and entered on the northern side.

It had taken three days to cover the 350 miles from Port Vila, with light winds from the southeast and calm seas. We had perfect sailing conditions, so Jamie was much happier.

The water was exceedingly clear, making the bottom look much closer than it was, so it was nerve-racking sailing over sharp coral bommies to enter the lagoon. The depth was about 30 feet where we anchored and I could see fish everywhere.

I grabbed my gear, dived off the back and came straight up with a good-sized fish on the spear. I called out to Jill, "How many of these do we need for lunch?"

"Maybe another two."

So down I went again and came straight up with another, then a third. I had caught lunch before my first cup of coffee in the lagoon.

Huon Island was covered in birds, mostly boobies, terns and frigate birds, all competing for nesting space.

Jamie and Sam with a fishing float near a booby's nest. Photo by J. Faulkner

It was the only land available to nest on and, being so far away from human habitation, they were quite safe. We had to be very careful when walking around the little islands to avoid stepping on the nests.

Jamie and Sam were absolutely enthralled by the big fluffy baby boobies, which were not afraid of us and allowed us to get close.

Some nests had quite large chicks almost ready to leave the nest. Photo by P. Faulkner

Everywhere we went, there were clouds of sea birds flying above the island, screaming at us to leave, so we didn't disturb them for long.

We were there for about four days and basically lived on fish that whole time. We didn't want to leave such an idyllic spot and I think the snorkelling was the best I've seen, in terms of colourful fish life and live coral. A real treat.

While wandering along the beach, I found a bottle with a message in it. I replied to the sender, a student from Vanuatu, but I never heard back.

We sailed across to the other side of the lagoon, which is probably five miles across and hadn't gone far when I hooked quite a good-sized fish. It was green and I thought "I'm not going to eat that!" I released it, dropped the line in again and caught another one.

I thought I'd better check our fish species book and found it was a commercial species in Queensland called a jobfish. We cooked the next one and it was delicious.

They're big, probably three feet long and quite solid. Although that was a lot of fish to eat, I couldn't resist putting the lines down again and 'bang!' another one, then another one, at which point I stopped fishing.

We anchored on the other side of the reef, not far from a big coral bommie and I really enjoyed snorkelling among the amazing fish living in and underneath it. In places the water was only 15 feet deep, so it was easy to access, but I didn't spear any fish there. We didn't need any more to eat with our freezer filled with fillets.

We had to be very careful when eating any fish that lived around reefs, especially large fish, as they could potentially be carrying ciguatera poison. For this reason we usually ate smaller reef fish. This rule didn't apply to pelagic species.

We headed for Chesterfield Reef, 270 miles away. The wind was between 10 and 15 knots, which suited us just fine.

If you're wondering how we washed ourselves on board the yacht, it depended on the availability of fresh water. If we didn't have a reliable source of fresh water, we would wash with salt water using detergent, which foamed up okay, then had a quick rinse off with a little fresh water from our tank. We could heat it using a solar shower bag that we tied to the mast, which worked very well, because we only used up half a gallon of water per person. If we were near a good water supply, we could fill up the solar shower and use three gallons per shower. Such luxury.

We settled into life on board and with a gentle sea running we could bake bread and do other daily tasks easily and safely. Life on board can be very difficult in rough seas and simple tasks like cooking can also be dangerous.

We were in fairly regular contact with a friend of ours in Hamilton, Cecil James, who was a ham-radio operator. He would pass on any messages to anybody we needed to contact in New Zealand. In fact, if we needed to speak directly with someone, he would put the microphone up to the phone receiver and juggle it from end to end depending on who was talking. That was quite difficult and one person would talk for a while before he switched the receiver.

This was primitive but effective, and we paid him back for all the toll calls within New Zealand later on. It was very comforting to know we weren't completely cut off and Cecil really enjoyed hearing firsthand about our adventures. He had a world globe which lit up and he would mark our position on it.

I spent some time on the ham radio in the evenings, because it was free to chat for as long as the signal was clear and occasionally the conditions were perfect.

One time I ended up chatting to someone in Berlin for half an hour, then someone from Moscow joined in. It was so clear, especially at night and it was as if they were on the yacht with me. They were astounded that I was in such a remote place.

Three days later we reached Chesterfield Reef, which includes Bellona Reef and quite a few separate islands. We found a pass to go through on the north side of the reef and anchored in 40 feet of crystal clear water.

The snorkelling was once again spectacular, with beautiful coral and fish. The whole archipelago is about 100 miles long and 50 miles wide, comprising 11 uninhabited islands and many reefs. The land area of the islands is less than six square miles and Bellona Reef is actually 120 miles southeast of Chesterfield.

Looking on the chart, there are several underwater mountain ranges running through the whole of the Coral Sea and those islands sit on top of the mountain ridges.

It was completely calm inside the lagoon and the surface was like glass, enabling Jamie and Sam to see right to the bottom from the boat.

That provided a lot of safe entertainment. I didn't see many reef sharks, but they are everywhere and I'm sure they were lurking.

I remember thinking at the time just how isolated we were, with no backup if something went wrong, which always made me a little nervous and extremely cautious.

It was a big lagoon, so we moved several times and checked out the diving in various locations. We ended up staying for six days, really enjoying the peace and quiet, blue sky and very calm seas. It was a cruiser's paradise. I managed to find a few crayfish, which were a delicious change.

As reluctant as we were to leave, we needed to keep heading towards Australia, so we sailed 150 miles to Kenn Reef. It took two days to get there, again with very gentle breezes between 10 and 15 knots from the southeast. Sailing on a beam reach, which is the fastest angle of sail, doesn't get much easier than that.

Kenn Reef is L-shaped and surrounded by very deep water, which plunges steeply close to the reef itself. There are a lot of other reefs and islands nearby, such as the Wreck Reefs and Cato Reef. The list goes on and on, as the Coral

Sea is a mass of reef complexes and tiny sand islands.

There was a very large boulder about eight feet high on the northern side of the reef. Despite the fact that it was conspicuous, there was a wrecked fishing boat rusting away nearby.

The only island is about 80 yards by 30 yards, with very little vegetation, and only about eight feet above the water. It was discovered in 1824 by Alexander Kenn, master of the ship *William Shen*, and it is in Australian territory.

While we were there, an Australian fishing boat came in. They were fishing out of large dinghies with hand lines, so they would race over to a coral bommie and catch what they could, then move on to the next one.

At night it was stunning, with fish creating streams of phosphorescence as they darted around in the water. It seemed almost magical.

Sometimes when sailing on a dark night, there was a long trail of phosphorescence behind the boat like a well-lit highway. It is caused by bioluminescent plankton in the water being stimulated by movement through the water and making them glow like glow worms.

This was our last anchorage before heading to Australia and we wouldn't be back, so I wanted to make the most of it.

We ended up staying at Kenn Reef for seven days, moving from place to place and anchoring a number of times. I caught a few crayfish and many different types of fish, including a couple more jobfish. The weather was very calm and it was almost glassy inside the lagoon at low tide, so it was another idyllic place to dive.

We finally set sail for Australia, aiming for Gladstone 230 miles away in virtually perfect sailing conditions with around a 15-knot southeasterly breeze.

We made very good progress and arrived in Gladstone with two tuna, on the 29th of June, one day before my birthday.

I didn't have a detailed chart of the channel coming into Gladstone, so we managed to go aground partway through the channel. Fortunately the tide was coming in and we hadn't dug in too hard, so we re-floated fairly easily.

A friendly yachtie, who had seen us stuck in the sand, came over later and loaned us a large-scale chart. We had been using a coastal chart, which doesn't have the large scale details for the ports.

It was good to be in Australia again, even though Gladstone is a very commercial port, with its aluminium smelter and lots of coal. Clearing customs and immigration at a smaller port like Gladstone is much more relaxed than the big ones.

It was also a good place for fixing things on the boat, with lots of engineering workshops and yachting supplies, so I could catch up on a few repairs and modifications. It was a real treat to have restaurants, shopping, movies and all the other trappings of civilisation, after being in the wild for so long.

I also got to celebrate my 38th birthday in style, with a couple of ice cold beers and a delicious meal at a Thai restaurant.

Chapter Fourteen

After three days of civilisation, topping up the water and diesel tanks and re-provisioning, we were ready to head north up the Great Barrier Reef. I was very keen to go back to Lady Musgrave Island and do some more diving there.

The conditions were perfect, with the wind from the southeast, still at about 15 knots.

I noticed a bit of die-off in the coral reef since we were there 10 years earlier, but there was still a lot of fish life in the marine reserve.

Jamie and Sam really liked the shallow water and snorkelling among the very colourful fish and coral. I just had to keep an eye on them if too many sharks congregated nearby. Sam would have been a delicious little morsel for their afternoon tea.

I've got two cling-ons! Photo by John Giddens

There were a number of stingrays and all manner of different varieties of fish. We weren't able to catch any of them, being in a reserve, so it was just as well we had stocked up on plenty of food. We were enjoying it so much that we didn't really want to leave, but after three days we started heading further north.

The next stop was the Heron Island marine reserve and dive resort. I knew what to expect, having visited 10 years earlier. It was very nice to be back again, but the anchorage at Heron Island was not very sheltered, so after two nights we headed up to Great Keppel Island.

We managed to catch a tuna on the way, so fish was back on the menu. I didn't carry a rifle on the boat on this trip because it was too much of a hassle dealing with customs officials, who didn't like us carrying guns on board. So we had to rely entirely on fishing and the occasional supermarket.

We were by now very comfortable with our lifestyle, having lived on board for over a year and becoming as self-sufficient as possible.

Great Keppel Island is quite large and has good elevation, so we enjoyed a good walk up the hill to check out the view. There are 17 white sandy beaches, with some of the greatest coral diversity in the Great Barrier Reef.

Jamie and Sam were fascinated by all the friendly turtles that congregate there and I thought I would show the kids my turtle-riding technique. I held onto one of the bigger turtles while his head was in the weeds and off we went at a great rate of knots.

I had forgotten how strong those turtles were, so I took a deep breath, pushed down with my hands, and down we went. I would pull up just in time so we could skim along above the coral, then rise to the surface so I could take a breath. The turtle certainly didn't need to come up for air that soon.

Jamie and Sam thought that was a great game and were pleased to see that I paid the turtle for the ride by removing the limpets from his back.

After three days at that perfect anchorage, we started moving north again. I was aware that the winds were consistently out of the southeast, which was going to make it easy to travel north but difficult to head south again, so we decided not to head any further north than the Whitsundays.

The next stop was Mackay, where we could shop at the supermarkets, top up with water and buy any other provisions we needed. I wanted to visit Hamilton Island, because they had quite a good aquarium and a dolphin enclosure that I knew the kids would really appreciate.

Hamilton Island is an exclusive and expensive resort, and the marina charges a lot. We worked out that the guys in charge of the marina would finish work about five pm, so we would motor into the marina at around six pm and tie up alongside another yacht. We could then spend the evening doing all the things that were available at the upmarket resort, including visiting the dolphins.

We would be sure to leave the marina at about seven am, well before the staff came back at eight. We would sail around to the other side of the island and spend the day on one of the beaches there, then come back and repeat the process the following night. It worked out well and cost us little.

Of course Jamie and Sam didn't want to leave, because they would miss their beloved dolphins, Buttons and Speedy, who were so tame we could actually pet them.

Photos by P. Faulkner

Hamilton Island has an international airport, so it was sometimes a bit disconcerting when a jet roared overhead and landed close by, but the gardens and the whole layout of the island were very attractive.

The next place we visited was Nara Inlet on Hook Island and, going ashore with my trusty screwdriver and hammer, I was able to get a large number of oysters. We had to cut some of them in half because they were too big to fit into our mouths.

The fishing was quite good there, too, so we spent a few days and managed to catch a few bream for dinner when I took Sam out for a ride in the dinghy. After we had been out for a few hours, Sam was sound asleep and I was getting pretty hungry. As we motored back towards *Maxine,* there was a delicious smell wafting from the boat. Freshly baked banana bread, my favourite! Jill had tried many different recipes and that was one of the best, along with glazed cinnamon swirls.

We then sailed to South Molle Island, which had a fairly laid-back resort and I pretended to be a guest in order to play a free round of golf. Off I went with a set of clubs to the nine-hole golf course and had a go. I'm no expert at golf, so I soon lost my ball. Determined to find my white number-three ball, I became obsessed with searching for it. All I could find was a yellow one and I realised that searching was not only a waste of time, but was also rather dangerous with snakes lurking in the rough areas. I gave up on my ball and carried on enjoying the picturesque golf course, looking out at *Maxine* anchored in the bay below.

Friday night on South Molle Island was Polynesian Night and they had a great Polynesian band plus a smorgasbord. The ticket for the smorgasbord was a plastic plate with a distinctive pattern on it, so when you had one of those plates, you just joined the queue and filled it with food.

South Molle Island is right at the opening of the Whitsundays and at the head of the bay is Airlie Beach, a popular tourist destination. Many yacht-hire companies and other tourist activities set off from Airlie Beach and it is close to many resort islands, so it's a great town for stocking up.

We could anchor close to the town, so it wasn't far to the shops and a large number of cruising yachties gather there in October. We decided to spend quite a bit of time in the area, with so much to explore on so many islands just offshore.

We were always on the lookout for yachts with kids on board to entertain Jamie and Sam, so we quickly made new friends and started hanging out on each other's boats.

Jill then decided she would take the kids home for a couple of weeks, to catch up with grandparents and family, so I invited a friend, Warwick Miller, to come over and spend a couple of weeks on the boat in the Whitsundays.

After showing Warwick around the sights of Airlie Beach, we headed for South Molle Island, where we had a round of golf, tried archery, went for a swim, soaked in the spa pool and finished up with the famous Friday night smorgasbord. Warwick said, "Peter, you are a real operator," and that name has stuck for decades.

The meal was up to its usual high standards, closely followed by some Polynesian music and dancing. South Molle Island was becoming a regular haunt for us, as we had to go right past it each time we went to stock up with water and provisions at Airlie Beach.

We headed out to Hook Island again and had some success with fishing and a lot of success with the very large oysters growing on the rocks in the bay.

Another hit with Warwick was rum slammers, a delicious combination of coconut water and rum. With this in mind, we took the mast from the dinghy. I had set up a sailing rig on my dinghy, with a rudder, keel, mast and sails. We tied a forked stick to the end of the mast, which at 14 feet was the ideal length, and went in search of green coconuts. As soon as they hit the ground, we cut them open and made a hole in the shell.

As we were doing this, a man asked, "What are you blokes doing?" Quick as a flash, I replied, "We're coconut inspectors – just checking the health of these palms."

Using a funnel, we would pour the coconut water into a one gallon container and put it in the fridge. "Rum o'clock" seemed to come around every evening at five and it was great having time to catch up with Warwick. We hadn't seen each other for some time and we used to flat together when I was 19, so our friendship went back quite a few years. Warwick had been working hard in the real estate industry in Auckland for some years and was really enjoying kicking back and doing very little.

I was able to introduce him to a number of other yachties we had befriended during our travels. It was a very sociable time and more and more yachts were gathering, as the Whitsunday annual regatta was about to commence.

On the Friday night, we decided to return to South Molle Island to repeat the previous week's activities, and of course I thrashed him at golf. Not that I was good, but I'd had more time to practise.

Two weeks flew by and my well-trained crew arrived back from New Zealand just in time for the start of the big regatta. There must have been at least 200 yachts gathered off Airlie Beach and a navy ship was anchored there as one of the markers for the fun race around the bay.

The race started with loud guns firing and we were off at about three knots in very light winds. I had built a spud gun out of a two-inch PVC tube and a XXXX beer can taped to one end with a hole punched in the bottom.

We would carefully pour in a cap full of methylated spirits, let it evaporate slightly in the sun, push in a potato and ram it about a foot down the tube with a winch handle. We would then angle the tube at the correct elevation and strike a lighter over the hole in the can. The vapour would explode and fire the spud for about 200 yards. That was certainly far enough to hit the neighbouring yacht's sail and hopefully drop the spud down their hatch.

We weren't the only ones to have a spud gun on board, so it was open slather on just about everyone, including the navy frigate. I felt a little nervous firing a spud gun at a navy ship with all those big gun barrels sticking out, but the only thing they retaliated with was their water cannon. Unfortunately it could travel a long way, so we worked hard to keep out of range. Those navy boys were very keen to hose us, so we had to keep our hatches firmly shut.

The fun and hilarity went on pretty much all day and of course we celebrated well into the night, with crews from the various yachts getting together on board the biggest boat.

Jamie and Sam thought this whole thing was just hilarious, as they had never seen such serious adults acting so stupidly. They would soon get used to it.

The Whitsunday Islands are very extensive, with many great anchorages to choose from, so I could see why they had become a base for so many resorts and different tourist activities, but we had a long way to travel to get to Mooloolaba, where we intended to spend the cyclone season. We had enjoyed many weeks with the other yachties, so it was hard to leave them and start heading south.

One of the yachts was called *Bydand*, sailed by Greg and Kristi, whose daughter Courtney enjoyed playing with Jamie and Sam:

Fun in the sand. Photo by P. Faulkner

Heading south was always going to be a challenge, as we were sailing pretty much straight into the prevailing southeasterly winds.

I noticed that the wind was always a bit lighter early in the morning, so we would set off at daybreak to try and get as far south each day as possible before the wind got up. It wasn't always possible, so some days we would just have to motor straight into the wind. That was a bit of a pain, as the waves stood up on end in the relatively shallow water.

Many other yachts were also heading south to get out of the cyclone area, so we often teamed up with one or two other boats and had some fun races on the way. We met up in whichever bays had the best shelter, which sometimes meant anchoring behind a headland, or in a bay on one of the outer islands. Of course I was always very keen to revisit our favourite diving islands.

We met two other yachts in Gladstone, and I noticed that there was a prawn trawler operating really close to the coast. I thought if he could catch prawns there, maybe we could catch some, too, using our bait net. I tied the net to the end of an oar and motored parallel with the shore with our powerful two-horsepower motor.

Greg helped by wading along the shoreline, where the water came up to his waist. To our huge surprise, when we pulled the net in we had about six pounds of prawns.

We all gathered on *Maxine* and feasted on the best tasting prawns I'd ever had.

A hungry crowd scoffing prawns. Photo by J. Williams

They don't come much fresher than that. We polished them off so quickly that we made another attempt to catch some more. While we were trawling, it gradually got darker, and, by the time we pulled the net in, there were a number of sea snakes in the net. We thought we'd better give up before we got bitten.

We came across a pod of humpback whales that seemed to be just lounging around inside the reef. I climbed the mast to get the best possible view and I could see the whole whale just below the surface. They are unbelievably huge creatures up close and this one would have been well over 60 feet long, dwarfing our 40-foot yacht. At one point a whale came clear out of the water and then breached, sending literally tons of water in a wave towards the boat. I had to hang on quite tightly to the mast, but it was a very exciting way to see them. There were even some little calves swimming alongside their mothers – a breathtaking sight.

By late November we were in Mooloolaba and decided that would be the best spot for us to spend the cyclone season. We found a great berth at the wharf marina that was handy to everything.

I got a job working for a new housing company in Maroochydore, so I had to go out and buy some decent work clothes, shoes and a bright yellow Renault, at great expense.

Sam, Jamie, Jill and me with our trusty Renault. Photo by J. Williams

The Renault had a tooth missing from the flywheel, so at the worst possible times it made an alarmingly loud screech. I would have to open the door with the car in second gear, then push very hard to make the motor turn over enough to clear the broken tooth.

Living in the marina was great socially, as we already knew a few of the yachts there, and we would often have barbecues on the beach or gatherings on each other's yachts.

I had never been quite happy with the performance of the self-steering gear* I built. A secondhand boat shop just happened to have a high-quality Monitor servo pendulum going cheap, as it was slightly damaged and a couple of parts were missing. So, I ordered the parts from the USA and made a new mounting system with hinges that allowed us to swing it out of the way to gain access through the transom door and then swing it back again and solidly mount it for use while sailing.

This gear is essential for long-distance sailing to avoid the sheer boredom of sitting in a cockpit, steering for hours every day. It also frees up the crew member on watch if they need to grab a drink or briefly leave the cockpit for something more urgent.

Chapter Fifteen

It seemed very strange to be back at work again after enjoying life at sea for so long. I gradually settled into selling houses and it was interesting dealing with all the different types of people who came along, and they would inevitably tease me about my Kiwi accent.

I couldn't help thinking how lucky they were to be able to buy a house for half the price we would pay in New Zealand. Australian houses were far superior and people were mostly on higher wages, so, from an economic standpoint, it was much easier for the average person to get ahead.

Alan and Sonia Little were the owners of Kewmore Homes, a small friendly company that I enjoyed working for. It was based in a subdivision in Maroochydore, where we had a few show homes for potential buyers to check out. Work was only a short drive from the Wharf

Marina in the yellow peril, my early model Renault stationwagon.

The beach being just across the road was also a big plus, with a children's playground, exercise equipment and coin-operated barbecues. Even in midwinter we would often be at the beach in shorts and T-shirts, having barbecues with friends, including Dave and Felicity Maire, whose son Glen was working at the local aquarium. Glen gave us virtually unlimited access to underwater entertainment only 100 yards from the boat.

They had an eight-foot-long basking shark that looked formidable, but they don't harm humans. While diving in the Pacific, I had been close enough to touch 10-foot-long basking sharks while they were snoozing on the ocean floor.

The aquarium's whitetip reef shark was six feet long and they can grow to about eight feet. They are probably the most common sharks in the Pacific and are very territorial, spending their whole life in one small area of a reef. They give birth to up to five pups annually or biannually.

Sometimes Jamie and Sam would spend an hour standing in the tunnel, mesmerised by these graceful sharks and an enormous manta ray swimming overhead. Glen delighted in hand feeding the sharks, much to the amazement of his audience. There were many other species, including moray eels, crayfish and beautifully coloured tropical fish of all shapes and sizes.

We were able to go into the aquarium after hours with Glen – so peaceful – and we could observe the behind-the-scenes operation, such as cleaning filters to keep the water quality perfect. The aquarium gave the children their first taste of the amazing underwater world I had experienced while diving.

Another of Jamie and Sam's favourite tourist sights was the massive crocodile at Australia Zoo.

Jill took the kids home for a couple of weeks, so that provided a great opportunity to get some jobs done on the boat while it was at the marina. Many of the jobs I needed to do were very messy and I had to remove panels inside the yacht to access the motor. I could make as much mess as I liked without little fingers and toes getting in the way.

One job that was impossible at sea was removing the 36-foot-long toe rails from the deck and laying them on the dock to be repaired and refurbished.

Jill and the kids returned to life on board a tidy yacht and the kids continued having fun with the other families in the marina.

One day after work, I dropped down the companionway ladder and Mum was sitting there! Jill and Mum had organised this surprise to coincide with my birthday, as Mum was flying home from her annual visit to the United States. She went every year to visit her mother who was in her 90s and it was easy to buy a ticket via Brisbane on the way back. It was great fun for all of us to be together on Mum's namesake *Maxine.*

Celebrating my birthday with Mum and the kids. Photo by J. Faulkner

Our stay in Mooloolaba was seven months altogether and it was going to be hard to leave our friends and give up the opportunity to sell more houses. I had sold 14 houses and was getting used to having a good income, which had allowed us to enjoy the city's entertainments, see the local sights and pay for the flights to New Zealand.

Mid-winter was a good time to head north to revisit some of the beautiful dive resorts we had enjoyed previously and catch up with friends along the way.

We didn't need extra crew to sail the Barrier Reef, so it was good to have a few months of family time in paradise.

When we reached Gladstone, Jill took the kids home to New Zealand to get back into normal life and my new crew arrived in Gladstone: Rex and Ruth James, from Hamilton, hadn't had any experience offshore sailing, but were both fit and keen.

I had known Rex since I was a baby, as his family had a farm next door to us when we lived near Palmerston North.

Also joining us was Shane Tobin, from Kaikohe. Shane was a friend of my brother Lewis and an experienced sailor who was handy at fixing things, being a plumber. During the trip, his skills proved useful on a number of occasions.

Ruth, Shane, Rex and me.

I was always a bit nervous before every ocean crossing and would go over the boat with a fine-tooth comb, checking for any weaknesses.

We spent a few days preparing by stowing the dinghy on deck, mounting the self-steering gear and clearing customs and immigration.

Departing Gladstone for New Caledonia, we had a great start with a 15-knot southerly, and the new self-steering gear was really coming into its own.

Ruth wrote later:

"We were very pleased to depart from Gladstone to escape the no-see-ums, tiny biting sandflies that caused us so much discomfort."

The crew couldn't believe how easy it was to steer the boat without touching the tiller, just very small adjustments to the self-steering gear. We were making a very accurate course, with fishing lines out as usual and it wasn't long before we landed a Spanish mackerel.

We quickly established a routine on the boat, taking turns cooking, doing the dishes, sail adjustments, baking the bread and all the other necessary chores. We also had to keep up with the weather using radio schedules.

Rex's father Cecil was a ham-radio buff, so we used him to pass on news and I could talk to Jill sometimes if he held the radio microphone up to the phone handset.

Ruth won the bread making competition, which was quite a feat, because we baked it in the pressure cooker to use less gas and avoid heating the cabin, as an oven would. The yeasty smell of bread baking was mouth-watering.

One day Rex was washing dishes in a bucket in the cockpit and when he'd finished, he tossed the rinse water overboard. "Clunk clunk clunk!" That was the sound of cutlery disappearing into thousands of feet of water, never to be seen again. Fortunately we had a few spoons and forks left.

Unfortunately, this blissful sailing was soon to be interrupted. Rex described it in a letter home to his children:

"We were in the middle of an electrical storm with almost continuous lightning and pelting rain. The wind was blowing 40 to 50 knots with 20 foot swells. The yacht was heeled over about 20 degrees and slamming into the waves."

Obviously we all survived the storm, but Rex told me many years later that had they known it would be so terrifying, they probably wouldn't have signed up as crew.

The last couple of days sailing to Noumea were almost perfect, so that was more fun. A booby bird decided to hitch a ride with us, resting on our radar dome to recover after the storm.

It looks as though I was wringing the booby's neck, but I was just trying to avoid getting pecked. Note the blade of the self-steering gear behind me. Photo by R. James

Ruth wrote about the calm after the storm:

"We made the most of having time on our hands and cooled off by diving overboard into the ocean. As soon as we hit the water we had

an overwhelming realisation that without that yacht we were doomed and each of us was happy to clamber back on board as soon as possible.

"Not one of us took a second dive.

"Not long after we were safely back onboard, we noticed a huge shark cruising gracefully by, so thankfully none of us was in the water at the time. It was also while becalmed that three whales, two adults and a young one, gave us a demonstration of their agility in the water. Listening to their noises and watching them spurting water before diving straight down was a magical experience that made the entire trip worthwhile."

We spent our first night in Noumea at the marina because it was free for one night, then we anchored in a little bay nearby after that to avoid paying $25 per day. Clearing customs and immigration took ages, but eventually we were free to explore.

We weren't at all surprised by the astronomical prices charged for virtually everything, as we had heard New Caledonia was expensive. I had stocked up well in Australia for that reason, but we still wanted fresh bread and vegetables. We thought it would be fun to eat out that first night, but the only reasonable deal we could find was a hamburger from a little truck in a nearby car park.

We stayed a few nights so I could have my roller furler sail and spinnaker professionally repaired, as it had torn during the trip from Australia.

We sailed north up the coast for a while, then out to a remote-looking reef complex. I was very surprised to find a large number of fish compared to Fiji, where the locals did a lot of fishing. In New Caledonia, the French Government provided the locals with everything they needed, so they weren't motivated to go fishing.

Shane and I were diving down looking underneath sponges and coral heads when suddenly we both spotted a huge crayfish. I could barely get in range with my spear gun and missed on my first shot. That scared the crayfish right across to the other side of the reef, where Shane was waiting with his speargun. It went back and forth until finally we managed to drag it out.

I couldn't believe how big it was, with such beautiful patterns on its shell. It was also delicious.

Shane and me with our prize. Photo by R. James

We had a long way to go and there wasn't a lot holding us in New Caledonia. After topping up with fresh water and vegetables, we headed south-southeast.

The following day saw us completely becalmed and we noticed a large tangled net floating on the surface. As we drew close to it, we saw some dorado swimming underneath. That reminded me how commercial fishermen set up what they call FADs, which are Fish Aggregation Devices, to attract small fish that in turn attract larger fish.

We trolled a lure right past the dorado, hoping to catch one, but they weren't even vaguely interested. After a few attempts we gave up and continued on our way.

The sea was glassy calm with no wind, so we motored most of the morning. It was necessary to motor for an hour each day as the fridge and freezer compressor ran directly off the motor, so it wasn't a waste of fuel if it kept our food cold.

A southeasterly breeze came up at lunchtime and we were soon sailing along at six knots. I noticed the size of the swells were increasing and they were coming from the north, which was unusual. According to the forecasts on our single sideband radio, a cyclone had developed north of the equator, so that explained the big swells. It was good to be making fast progress, averaging about 150 miles a day.

One of the things I enjoyed most about doing ocean crossings was the interaction of the crew, who were pushed together into a very tight environment, so we had to get on well. There was no escaping if things weren't going your way and I'd heard many tales over the years of people having terrible crews. Fortunately I usually had a sixth sense about who to take on board, because it can really affect the mood of the whole trip.

Our next stop was Norfolk Island and as we approached its steep cliffs, we could see large swells coming in on the northern side and the wind was coming from the southwest. This made it quite difficult to get a really sheltered anchorage anywhere on Norfolk Island, but we eventually dropped anchor on the northern side. It was very deep with a large swell breaking onshore, which was very disconcerting, but we had no choice.

We decided the only way we were going to get ashore was to leave one person on board as anchor watch while the other three visited the island.

A concrete wharf jutted out from the steep cliffs and there was a manual winch that could be swung out over the water to pick up goods and small boats.

Gantry lifting a local boat with Maxine *anchored well offshore.*
Photo by R. James

The problem was that the swells were completely breaking over the wharf at times and then smashing on the rocks behind. It was pretty scary, but after watching a number of different sized waves come in and break, I chose the smallest wave to take the dinghy in close to the steps.

Rex and Ruth leapt off and raced up the steps before the next wave came and I zipped back out to deeper water, watching the next few waves smash on the rocks.

A couple of locals swung the winch out over the edge of the wharf for me. I had attached the harness to the dinghy that we usually used to lift it onto the deck of the yacht. I needed to get the dinghy in behind the winch, swing it around facing out to sea and then quickly hook the winch onto the harness.

I watched a number of big swells come in and could see that after five or six swells there was sometimes a gap, so I aimed for one.

As soon as I hooked on, they whisked me up to safety as another huge swell thundered under the dinghy. The winch swung the dinghy, with me somehow still on board, onto the wharf and we all carried the dinghy away as close to the cliffs as possible.

The waves smashing on the wharf. Even with the dinghy that far away, it still got damaged by a wave. Photo by R. James

One of the locals who helped us with the dinghy was John Buford, aka "Buff" and he took us under his wing, insisting that we go back to his place for a visit. We squeezed into his rusty old Corolla and struggled up the steep track to his house, where he very kindly made us lunch.

Buff was very proud of his ancestry, as he was descended from the Christian family that was involved in the mutiny on the *Bounty* in 1789.

He was an avid wood turner, so he wanted us to have a go too. I ended up making a model sheet winch out of some beautiful hardwood that he had lying around and I still have it.

He offered us his 'limousine' for a spin around the island. We started our tour at the penal colony, a frightening place with a very dark history. It was one of the most brutal jails in the world at the time.

Norfolk Island is very small, one of three islands with a total of only 35 square miles. The climate is almost perfect, not too hot and not too cold, and Kingston is the main town.

Polynesians were the first to settle Norfolk Island, but they had already departed when Great Britain settled it as part of its 1788 colonisation of Australia and the island served as a convict penal settlement. In June 1856, descendants of the *Bounty* mutineers were relocated from Pitcairn Island.

We decided we would stay one more night to give Shane a chance to see the island. All of us went ashore because the swell had decreased and *Maxine* was safely anchored.

Buff entertained us again and we will never forget his amazing hospitality and trusting us with his limousine for another day.

Shane, Buff, Rex and me. Photo by R. James

After surviving another island tour, we set off with a 15-knot southeasterly breeze towards New Zealand.

I was surprised and pleased to see a large flock of fairy terns just as we were leaving Norfolk Island, as they were becoming quite rare. Their flight pattern was very erratic and the way they flitted about with their forked tails was quite distinctive. Only about 50 fairy terns remained in New Zealand in the wild at the time and weighing only two ounces means they are small and vulnerable.

As we headed south it was getting cooler day by day as we left the tropics and entered the temperate region.

A sperm whale appeared in the distance, so we headed towards it. Humpback whales are fairly common, but I'd never seen a sperm whale up close. We managed to get reasonably close and when it disappeared we carried on our way.

It wasn't long before we hooked a bonito, also known as a skipjack tuna. It is quite a dark-fleshed fish, not as tasty as some, but it cooked up quite well into a curry.

It was great to get back into a routine on a relatively long passage. The crew relied on each other for entertainment and sat around talking for hours and hours on end, adjusting the self-steering gear and watching the horizon for ships, and one day just rolled into the next surprisingly quickly.

We were able to get reasonably good weather reports on the single sideband radio and would listen on fixed schedules where yachts were checking into their home base in New Zealand. The South Pacific Cruising Rally had boats travelling in all directions, so that was a useful channel to listen to. We could tell what sort of weather they were having 100 to 200 miles to our west and, as the weather always came from that direction, we knew what to expect the next day. That was very handy as it would allow us to get our sails down long before a storm hit.

The prevailing southwesterly breeze was gentle, so it was very relaxing not having to change the sails for days.

I hadn't played any music professionally for several years, so it was fun to get the guitar out on occasion and play some well-known songs. None of my crew were musicians that time, but they enjoyed humming along.

As we approached New Zealand, the weather was a lot cooler and the breeze was more fickle, getting up to 30 knots at one point, which was a bit uncomfortable, but it didn't last long. Without too much drama we were home after five days' sailing.

My life was about to change considerably as I got back to work again after two-and-a half-years spent mostly cruising.

Chapter Sixteen

The first thing I remember about being back in Auckland was being driven along the motorway from the marina to Jill's brother's house.

After travelling mostly at six or seven knots for two-and-a-half years, 60 miles per hour was absolutely terrifying! My body had slowed right down and adjusted to the different pace of life, so it seemed like we were screaming along way too fast. I was hanging on for grim death.

I landed another job quite soon after we got home, working for Green and McCahill Properties.

Just another hard day at the office. Photo by M. Long

Two Irish partners had founded the company many years before with just a pick, shovel and wheelbarrow and eventually bought up large tracts of residential land around Auckland. They developed subdivisions and built houses, so part of my job was selling sections and houses.

I enjoyed working there, but needed my own project, so I started building a house during free weekends and evenings. That really stretched me and led to a slipped disc in my back. I was out of action for some months and stuck in bed for the first three weeks. It was rather frustrating.

Four-year-old Sam decided that he wanted to learn more maths during that time, so he set about learning all the times tables while I was a captive audience. I made up cards with the times tables on them and when he got one wrong, I would put it aside and come back to it later. It wasn't that long before he had mastered the 12 times table.

When he finally started school aged five, the teacher took him to the headmaster, thinking there was something strange about this child who already knew the 12 times table. He became a very good mathematician, so all that early one-on-one study must have paid off.

I belonged to the Panmure Yacht Club, which often had rallies where a number of boats would go out on a cruise for the weekends, especially on public holidays.

One of the favourite spots to go to was Kawau Island, which is right at the top end of the Hauraki Gulf. The mansion house, built in the 1840s for the mine superintendent, was bought by Governor George Grey in 1862.

When we went there, the mansion house was an interesting museum to visit and there were still plenty of wallabies and noisy but beautiful peacocks. The wallabies kept the grass so short it looked like someone had mown it, very unusual for a wild island like that. It was a great anchorage and we would get together at the yacht club and have barbecues, go fishing and have a few beers.

There are plenty of other islands to visit near Auckland, such as Motuihe, Rangitoto, Motutapu and Rakino. These islands form an effective buffer zone and protect Auckland's inner harbour from the open ocean.

Panmure Yacht Club was very well setup for yacht maintenance, so they could easily haul

10-ton *Maxine* out of the water. I needed to work on the underwater side of the boat every year to keep up the antifouling. It was also very helpful to have some experienced people with engineering skills who were happy to help with projects I wasn't quite up to.

I got involved in racing on a Friday night at the rum races, where the winners won a bottle of rum. I was sailing on a Farr MRX 30 and there were about 11 of that class of boat, which were an ideal training design.

A lot of the America's Cup sailors would take them out for practice and the skipper of the boat I was on, Colin Maddren, had been quite successful in the Olympic Games racing dinghies, so we had quite a crack team.

I learned the finer points of sail trimming from them and when we had America's Cup team members on board, I would take a back seat, sit on the rail as ballast and do as I was told, for a change. It was great fun and I enjoyed learning about the tactics of racing, especially when we won our bottle of rum, but I much preferred cruising.

I also raced on *Hydroflow,* a fast 49-foot offshore racing yacht with 13 crew. In one of the races, all of us were sitting along the upwind rail doing just over 20 knots, which felt very fast to me, when a 60-foot yacht called *Georgia* overtook us easily.

The race went past Motutapu Island, and before I knew it we were already at Tiritiri Matangi, before racing back to Auckland.

Hydroflow won two Auckland to Noumea races and her owner, Ron Brittain, said she maintained 24 knots for about 12 hours.

He was a bit concerned about a noise the keel made at that speed when it started vibrating. It was a drop keel, which was perhaps a little loose in its housing and I hate to think what would have happened if it had snapped when a long way offshore.

Thankfully I wasn't involved in that race but it was very exciting sailing on such a fast racing yacht and quite a change from cruising along at five or six knots.

Auckland is a great location to sail out of because the huge Hauraki Gulf is full of islands, most with good anchorages no matter which direction the wind is coming from.

Every Christmas we would sail the 60 miles to Great Barrier Island for about a month of fishing, snorkelling and spending time with a number of friends who lived on the island. They had various businesses, such as a plant nursery, cafe and mussel farm.

We treated the mussel farm as our fish supermarket, because schools of small fish shelter under the floats and attract kingfish and other large species. I would snorkel up and down the rows, patiently awaiting the best moment to dive down and spear one of the bigger fish.

When I hit one, it was absolute chaos as the fish would wrap itself around the ropes and lines and get completely tangled. It was then a matter of waiting until the fish was exhausted, to dive down and safely put it out of its misery. This was a very reliable way to catch fish, as well as great fun for me.

Kingfish grow even bigger than this one, but I wouldn't be game to shoot one as I might drown trying to hold it. Photo by J. Faulkner

We could also collect as many mussels as we wanted from the main anchor lines, which couldn't be harvested commercially.

One night we set the net and caught five trevally by daybreak. I was skinning the fish and noticed that when I threw the shiny skins overboard, about five kingfish came up to investigate.

I called to Sam: "Quick! Pass me the spear gun!"

I put a piece of skin on the end of a rod and told him to hang it over the side and jiggle it up and down. "Not too deep, come up a bit so I can reach the fish."

Sure enough, one came right up to the piece of skin and 'zonk!' I got it! But what a fight that was. Eventually I got it on board and we had blood and guts all over the cockpit, but we weren't complaining.

Great Barrier is a very unspoilt island so we would go on lots of bush hikes. There are numerous tracks, some of which took us to old kauri dams. In the 1920s, they used to cut down those huge trees for their very valuable timber and store them in a big dam made of logs. When enough water built up under the kauri, they would knock a huge pin out to release the timber, hurling it down the stream to hopefully reach the sea. It usually seemed to work. The kauri logs would then be tied together to form a barge and towed to a sawmill on the mainland.

There were quite a few rabbits on the island so we would sometimes take the .22 into the bush and bring one back for dinner. Sam was very keen to shoot one, but the gun was too heavy for a five-year-old.

Jamie didn't know we had been shooting rabbits, so when she found out her 'chicken' dinner was actually rabbit, she suddenly lost her appetite.

I also had my eye on the wild cattle in the bush, but decided that was a bit ambitious, especially as we couldn't store that much meat. I left them for the locals.

Great Barrier Island was definitely the best place for an extended sailing holiday near Auckland, so we went there almost every year for 20 years. The northern end of Great Barrier Island was completely uninhabited and covered in bush, with interesting valleys to explore by walking up the streams.

The western side of the island is quite well protected from ocean swells and we would sometimes do a trip right up around the northern end to the Pinnacles, then on to beautiful Whangapoua Beach on the eastern side.

We attempted to get ashore there, through the breakers, but the dinghy flipped in the surf. We all fell in and the kids were floundering around, but of course they had life jackets on. Nobody was harmed but the outboard went underwater, so I took it off the dinghy, carried it to a stream at the far end of the beach and submerged it in fresh water to get rid of all the salt. I then stripped it down, emptied the carburettor, cleaned everything up and it went again.

It wasn't the first time I'd dunked that outboard in seawater, so it was obviously very resilient and I always kept it well lubricated and sprayed with CRC.

There was a graveyard on the headland at Whangapoua Beach and we learned that one of the worst shipwrecks in New Zealand's maritime history occurred near Miner's Head. About 140 people drowned when the SS *Wairarapa* hit rocks there in 1894 and some of them were buried in the graveyard.

We took a trip out to Arid Island, which is very small and has been farmed with sheep and cattle. There is a small bay with a gorgeous little beach, where about four yachts can anchor. Some impressive rock formations with archways were just wide enough for the dinghy and we squeezed into some narrow caves to see beautiful gold and blue rocks.

Many of our Panmure Yacht Club friends would travel to Great Barrier in the summer holidays. We spent a lot of time with one particular couple up there, David and Gwen Bott on their trimaran *Pengwen*.

Photo by D. Bott

David and I have had many adventures over the years, sharing our passion for sailing, diving and fishing.

Another highlight was the annual Fitzroy Mussel Festival, which attracted dozens of boats to Fitzroy Yacht Club. It was perched high on a hill in the bush and overlooked the spectacular harbour.

They cooked mussels in every conceivable way, so we sampled mussels in burgers, fritters, pickles and soups.

That summer they had the wonderful Rick Bryant Blues Band and I was asked to play for an hour before they started. I did an acoustic set on guitar and a talented local singer joined me with vocal harmonies.

After all that fun, they put me to work behind the outdoor bar for the rest of the night. I managed to escape and had a few dances in between pouring beer, so it wasn't all work and no play.

The time seemed to fly by and with a tinge of sadness we had to head back to civilisation for school and work.

Not long after leaving Fitzroy Harbour, we came across a huge pod of bottlenose dolphins, some of them cavorting and playing near the bow. I did a high-pitched whistle, the dolphins squeaked and the kids squealed. Jamie and Sam were harnessed on, so there was no danger of them falling overboard with all the excitement.

With the swish of the bow wave and creaking of the rigging, it was quite a symphony. The dolphins leapt well clear of the water and looked like they were having a great time. I have enjoyed the company of those wonderful creatures many times, but it is always exciting when they join us and it was a perfect end to our summer holiday.

Chapter Seventeen

Life was very busy and two-and-a-half years flew by, then it was time to head north again to Fiji. This time it didn't take anywhere near as much effort to get the boat ready for the offshore trip.

My friend John Newton was keen to sail up with us, along with my sister Jean and another friend from a music club I belonged to, Katie Horwood.

That was quite a mixed crew and I wouldn't normally go without another experienced crew person, but there wasn't anyone available. I was confident in John's innate ability to cope with most situations and it's amazing how quickly an intelligent crew can meld into a team. This crew was an interesting blend of personalities.

Day one saw us sailing up the coast of the North Island with a 15-knot southwesterly breeze, a perfect direction on the beam quarter.

That was my favourite point of sail, heeled slightly to one side by the wind crossing the back quarter of the yacht, whereas sailing directly downwind can cause an uncomfortable side-to-side roll.

By late in the day, the wind had picked up a little and was probably more like 18 knots. I suspected it might increase, so we put two reefs in the mainsail, which is fairly hard to do when you're going downwind, because the pressure makes it hard to get the sail down. But we managed that, then furled the headsail more and were still making good progress at six or seven knots.

We had not long cleared the top of New Zealand when we caught our first tuna, a large yellowfin – they are delicious. We were lucky to catch one so early in the trip because we often did long trips and caught nothing.

By the following morning the wind was over 20 knots and the seas kept gradually building, day after day, over the next six days. We started to surf on the huge swells, which was a bit disconcerting and potentially hazardous.

We often had to disconnect the wind vane steering system and steer by hand as we were afraid that we might broach, which would be disastrous. John remembers straining on the tiller and wondering if it would snap.

Night time on the yacht is quite spectacular, with no other light around and the stars so clear and bright.

John described one of his experiences on night watch:

"*I was sitting in the cockpit when all of a sudden a little splash of water hit my face. I wondered what it was, then it happened again and again. Flying fish were flying right across the boat and I could feel drops of water dropping from their fins. It got quite frightening because some of the bigger ones flying at that speed might have knocked me out. Every now and then one would land on the deck, flapping helplessly.*"

In the morning we gutted and cleaned them, split them open, then salted and dried them in the sun.

By day three the wind had got up to about 25 knots and the seas had continually built to the point where they were probably around 30 feet, so we had to be careful.

At times we would get up to 15 knots surfing down the front of those waves, then slow right down in the trough, before repeating the process. It didn't pay to look behind us, because the great mountains of water looming up were pretty scary. Just as they looked like they were going to break, the boat would lift up and over and away we'd go again. That was pretty exhilarating sailing and it was great to be making such fast progress.

I really appreciated the roller furling headsail, a wonderful invention that saved us having to go up on deck in rough conditions. It was much safer to reduce the headsail from the cockpit.

By then we only had half the headsail out and half the mainsail, but still maintained about seven knots.

On day six we arrived at South Minerva Reef and it was a big relief to be tucked inside in perfectly calm water.

I'd forgotten just how spectacular the diving was there and we rested for two days and enjoyed the incredibly clear water that was teeming with fish. After the fairly hectic sail up from New Zealand, it was a relief to chill out for a change.

The wind had eased and swung around to the prevailing southeasterly trade winds at around 12 knots. With the gentle breeze, the rest of the trip was much more relaxing and warmer as we headed north.

Our first sighting of Fiji was Matuku Island, one of the southernmost islands in the Lau Group, which stretches down to about 500 miles from Tonga.

Not long after we sighted the island, we got into a large school of dorado. There must have been well over 100 of them. They are known to gather in large schools when they are spawning, usually in fairly shallow water.

The fertilised eggs sink to the bottom where they attach to rocks and seaweed. Dorado are quite spectacular with their green, blue and gold colours flashing in the sun when they jump out of the water. Their name comes from the Spanish word for gold.

We dropped the sails, started the motor and went around the school in a large circle with two lines trailing out the back. We always used a light rope that is easy to grip with leather gloves. It was attached to the boat with some loops of car inner tube to take up the shock when a large fish hit the line.

On the end of the rope we used 350-pound monofilament and a short wire trace with twin high-tensile stainless hooks. We weren't sport fishing, just trying to catch something to eat, and it is a lot quicker to haul them in on a rope than with a rod and reel.

We hooked one pretty quickly and hauled it in, but just as we got it near the boat it leapt out of the water, thrashed around and dislodged the hook.

We soon had another on the line and because we still had the self-steering gear in the water, we couldn't haul it in through the open back door of the transom without damaging the wind vane. So, instead we had to lift the fish up the side of the boat, giving it a much better chance to escape.

We hooked 16 of those big fish, got eight of them to the boat, but only managed to land four. The cockpit was an absolute shambles with blood everywhere, but it was pretty exciting fishing and we then had plenty of fish in the freezer.

Dorado have an unusual shape and the males, with their square heads, can grow up to four feet long. They are delicious and, although it took a long time to fillet, vacuum pack and load them into the freezer, it was well worth the trouble.

Knowing how difficult it is to clear in with all the officials in Suva, we decided to clear in at the old capital, Levuka. Immigration and customs were much more laid back and easygoing there, so clearing in was actually a pleasure and we spent a couple of days enjoying the quaint old town, especially the restaurants and ice-cold Fiji Bitter.

I heard of an island nearby called Leleuvia, "the island of love", which is actually a small sand cay and only about 10 feet out of the water. We headed around the outside of the surrounding reef and found the pass to get through. On one side of the sand cay there was just enough room for two boats to anchor and we nearly always had it all to ourselves. To keep fit, I would run around the island. It only took 10 minutes so I did five laps.

We had a lot of fish on board and I wasn't interested in cooking all the time, so I thought I would try selling them to the resort. It was run by Emosi and he was happy to take the fish in return for some meals.

It was a very sociable island, mainly for backpackers, and we would all sit around on grass mats drinking kava and singing and playing guitar until all hours.

Left to right: Emosi, me and Steve.

It was great to be with some other musicians, many of whom were resort staff, as well as my friend Kate who had sung with me at the music club in Auckland.

Emosi was a true entrepreneur and was always trying to talk me into joining him with some sort of business scheme. I was a bit reluctant as I wasn't supposed to be earning any money in Fiji, but it wasn't long before I was taking tourists on the occasional sunset cruise to see whales or dolphins. We would get a few takers at $20 each.

I also took five paying guests on an extended cruise and Emosi joined the crew. It was great fun doing a tour around Ovalau, then to Levuka, but some officials spotted us with the extra passengers and realised they were probably paying guests.

I didn't have a permit and Emosi's powers of persuasion didn't get us off the hook. However they didn't fine us on the condition that we returned directly to Leleuvia. We actually took two nights to get back, stopping at resorts where Emosi knew the owners. The resort owners didn't report us, as they clearly had a vested interest in welcoming us and our guests.

Another activity was walking along a sandbank that was exposed at low tide. The walk took you all the way out onto the reef, investigating the little creatures stranded in the rock pools that we could usually only see while snorkelling. We could walk for miles, but it was important not to get too distracted and to return well before the tide came in.

Some of the staff who worked on the island lived on Moturiki, which is the next island between Leleuvia and Ovalau. They invited us to the village for church the following day. I was very keen to go because I knew how good the singing would be and looked forward to hearing some beautiful harmonies.

We took one of the local boats over to Moturiki, which was fun in itself. I really enjoyed the church service, not that I appreciated the endless ranting of the pastor in Fijian, but the singing was fantastic.

Straight after church we all gathered at one of the houses and sat around on grass mats at a very long table. There were around 20 people and we shared the traditional Fijian lovo, which is cooked in the ground. Sweet potato, taro, cassava and, of course, the raw fish dish kokoda, which is, fish soaked in lemon juice until it is 'cooked' and flavoured with coconut cream, onions and tomatoes.

Another of my favourites was palusami – taro leaves cooked in coconut cream. It was all delicious and we sat around chatting, drinking tea and soaking up some normal village life.

They made us feel like part of their family. That evening, back on Leleuvia, we sat around on grass mats, playing guitar and singing along after dinner.

Music and kava. Photo by J. Newton

With kava and a couple of quiet beers it was very relaxing and my crew had their first experience of the real Fijian way of life. This is quite different from the touristy western side of Fiji.

We sailed to Suva on the outside of the reef, cruising along with the stereo going and singing along loudly to Tom Petty's "Into the Great Wide Open", then U2 with some great drumming. As we were coming up to the entrance into Suva Harbour we were only halfway through the song, all drumming away. We didn't want to turn into the harbour entrance until the song had finished, so at the last possible second the song ended and we did the sail changes necessary for the 90 degree turn.

On another trip from Leleuvia to Suva, we decided to sail inside the outer reef. There is a narrow channel between that and the inner reef, which are both large colonies of coral. There was a nice, light, following breeze so I decided to set the spinnaker, but soon after we set it, the wind got up slightly and we were going faster and faster, probably around seven knots, with razor-sharp coral zipping past on both sides.

It was quite disconcerting and when I realised that I didn't actually have room to turn the boat around to drop the spinnaker, we just had to hang on for grim death and keep going. We were winding in and out of coral heads without much clearance on either side, with our speed still increasing.

I realised the only thing I could do was keep going and eventually we popped out into the main harbour of Suva. With a great sigh of relief, I spun the boat around into the wind and dropped the spinnaker. The crew thought it was a hilarious adventure, but I didn't think it was quite so funny. It was actually quite dangerous and I would never do that again.

Suva, the largest city, has everything you can imagine, including the University of the South Pacific, movie theatres, nightclubs, restaurants and the Royal Suva Yacht Club, which was full of expats from around the world who drank there regularly. It is quite a pleasant place to eat and pass some time and, having been there before, I played music with some locals I knew.

It was great to have a taste of city life, see the latest movies, go to a nightclub, listen to some good music and eat in a huge variety of restaurants.

Being on the eastern side of Fiji, "Soggy Suva" gets a lot of rain generated by the surrounding hills, so we didn't want to spend much time there. The crew all needed to catch a flight home to Auckland, so they caught a bus to Nadi Airport, and Jill and the kids arrived the same day. We had a complete change of crew.

We became friends with a lovely Indian family from the yacht club and they invited us home for a curry. Of course we couldn't resist that and Jill took the opportunity to learn how to cook a real curry. I couldn't believe the difference between an authentic home-made Indian curry and those we had been eating in restaurants. There was just no comparison, but it was a bit spicy for Sam and Jamie.

They were now six and eight years old respectively, so we used the great education course from the New Zealand Correspondence School.

The students hard at work. Photo by P. Faulkner

They supplied us with all the material for the next year or so of school, and, each morning for three hours, Jill taught Jamie and I taught Sam. That was enough schooling for the day, because it was intensive one-on-one, so then we could spend the rest of the day having adventures.

Before heading east, we enjoyed lots of children's movies, eating at restaurants we hadn't visited and stocking up on provisions. There were also a few bundles of kava on board this time from the fresh vegetable market.

It's not always possible to just head in whichever direction you want in a yacht. Because we wanted to head east and the tradewinds were southeasterly, we had to do a lot of tacking. That involved heading well south on one tack, then northeast on the next tack. Of course we had to cover twice the distance to do that, but it was worth a hard day's sailing to visit the quieter eastern region.

One of those peaceful spots was Thangalai Island, not far from Leleuvia and Moturiki. A family lived on that very small island and they welcomed us with open arms, especially as we had two playmates for their children.

They also appreciated our help gathering produce from the gardens, cutting bananas and digging up taro and cassava. We then prepared the lovo together to cook it all in the ground. Thangalai is a small sand cay and it was fun to just kick back and get to know the family.

Jamie remembers that at low tide we could walk from the main island across rocks and reef out to a small rocky island. She found a sea snake out there and lots of other creatures.

Occasionally sea snakes would bask in the sun on *Maxine's* lolly scoop. I would flick them off, but once they had found that warm spot they kept coming back. We had to be careful before stepping onto the lolly scoop.

We did a trip with a local family to Moturiki on Sunday to enjoy the singing in church again. Our children were quite impressed with all the music.

Life in a small village was becoming much more familiar to us now, with chickens running around, the occasional pig and lots of children everywhere. Almost all the villagers spoke fluent English, apart from some of the elderly, who only spoke Fijian.

They wanted to know all about our lives as much as we wanted to know about theirs and the women and children absolutely loved hanging out with Jamie and Sam.

It was easy to spend quite a lot of time in the villages and being musical was a huge advantage in getting to know the locals. They practically adopted anyone who got out the guitar and started singing along with them.

The kava bowl was usually brought out and we sat around on mats, playing music, drinking and chatting into the night.

After spending about a week on both Thangalai and Moturiki, we sailed around the other side of Ovalau to Levuka and stocked up at the supermarket, then headed to Makogai Island.

We had visited five years earlier and watched them breeding turtles and giant clams. The staff remembered us and we picked up where we had left off and it wasn't long before I was kitted up with scuba gear to scrub clam cages on the seafloor.

This time, Jamie and Sam, at eight and six, could really enjoy snorkelling above me, watching the whole process. Hundreds of little fish gathered to feed on all the algae and other food I was disturbing while cleaning the cages.

It was great to see that some of the turtles had grown quite big and were almost ready to be released into the wild to hopefully repopulate the area.

Sam and Jamie with turtles. Photo by P. Faulkner

I wanted to visit more of the Lau Group, where only 19 of the 60 islands were inhabited, so we headed south to Lakeba Island. Lakeba is known as a chiefly island, where many famous Fijian chiefs came from. One was Ratu Sir Kamisese Mara, who was the first prime minister of Fiji and probably the longest serving, from 1920 to 2004.

On our first visit we would always present kava to the local chief. They take their kava ceremonies very seriously, as it is one of the traditional ways of greeting visitors. After the ceremony we were permitted to wander anywhere on the island.

We had caught a tuna on the way there and the locals were very pleased when we gave it to them to cook in the lovo that night.

The following day I was invited to go fishing in one of their small fibreglass boats. They used Yamaha 60-horsepower outboards, as did almost everyone in the islands, probably because they were the most reliable engines and simple to keep running. The fibreglass boats they used were all made from the same mould, about 20 feet long and very narrow, so they were quite fast.

We headed out to their favourite fishing spot and did quite well, catching some reef fish, coral trout and various different species. That evening we had kokoda, raw fish in coconut cream, and it was delicious, as always.

We had heard about Lakeba Island's limestone caves and hired a guide to take us on a snorkelling tour through some of the best. The water was surprisingly cool and the limestone formations were stunning and had absolutely spectacular colours.

As we were much further south, it was obvious that there had been some intermarriage with Tongans and their way of life was slightly different, so we got to experience another culture. The Tongan influence showed in the language, clothing and architecture, which featured rounded houses rather than the square-ended ones elsewhere in Fiji.

In the 1990s archaeologists discovered a massive fortress built around a thousand years ago and large enough to house over 2000 people. It was believed to be a bulwark against Tongan invaders.

It was about 70 miles to Totoya Island, so we needed to leave early to arrive in daylight. With a 15-knot southeasterly breeze, we had a smooth sail and even caught a dorado on the way.

Our timing was perfect and we arrived with plenty of daylight to sneak in through a pass late in the afternoon. We anchored off the village of Tovu on the eastern side of the bay and it wasn't as shallow as we had hoped, so we had to anchor in deep water with a muddy bottom. This was a bit disconcerting because we might drag anchor, so the following day we shifted to a more secure anchorage.

We went ashore to make sevusevu by presenting kava root to the island's chief. Some islands are very casual about the presentation, while others are more formal and stick to their traditional ways. This time we had quite an official type of presentation and they wore Tongan-style woven mats, which we had never seen before in Fiji.

The whole island is less than 11 square miles of actual land and there are no roads or vehicles, which is quite unusual. Their children had never even seen a bicycle, but we decided not to bring our bike ashore because there were no roads to ride it on. A supply ship called the *Lau Trader* came once a month with supplies and passengers from Suva, so they weren't completely isolated.

A really good way of getting to know the locals is to help them with some of their broken machines, such as outboards and generators. It was fun hanging out with them and repairing lots of things.

We moved on to another village called Ketei, just north of Tovu, where there was a much better anchorage. There was also no shortage of things that needed fixing, so we spent more time doing that than digging in the gardens as we would normally have done.

The island was quite poor and we were pressed upon to supply all sorts of things, including medical supplies that we didn't have much of. We also traded shorts and T-shirts and other things we'd bought from opshops for that purpose.

One of the families invited us home for lunch and they served turtle meat. They knew it was illegal to catch turtles and they didn't want us to take any photos, but they explained that the turtles had never been overfished there, so they were plentiful.

They only ate one a couple of times a month, so their turtles were less likely to become endangered than a lot of other areas in Fiji. I must say I did taste the turtle and it was absolutely delicious, very much like pork, but vaguely fishy.

The Lau Group has a low population that is declining because there is no work. A lot of young people want to leave and go to the cities for better pay and more opportunities and this leads to a lot less pressure on the fishing population.

After about three weeks of immersing ourselves in a lovely slow pace of life in the Lau Group, we found a spell of settled weather to set off on the 130-mile trip back to Suva.

We left at midday, hoping to arrive in daylight and after a perfect sail downwind we arrived at 10 the following morning.

Chapter Eighteen

In Suva, we did the usual re-provisioning, eating out and watching movies. All of these things were greatly appreciated after spending so long in the wilderness – not that we lacked any luxuries, with good facilities and plenty of comforts on the yacht.

We were able to live like kings in Suva, as we hadn't spent any money for about five weeks. Our currency in the islands was mostly clothes we had bought in New Zealand opshops specifically for trading. We didn't need cash much, but if we did the income from our Auckland rental property was still going into our account.

Suva was a useful place to do any repairs, as I knew quite a few locals who were involved in engineering and welding, or knew where to get the components I needed. They were all very generous and helpful.

A few days later, we started heading to the western side of Viti Levu, the main island. We anchored overnight in a small harbour about 20 miles west of Suva.

The next morning, while motoring out towards a narrow coral pass with a reasonable swell breaking on either side, the motor died. We were very lucky that we hadn't entered the pass yet, as I was able to quickly turn the boat around and drop the anchor. After a lot of investigation, I discovered there was water in the fuel. I could see it in the fuel filter bowls and wondered how on earth it could possibly have got in there. I kept searching and discovered that the mast had filled up with water to quite a height. The drainage holes I had made at the bottom of the mast weren't quite big enough to cope with the dirt and whatever else had built up inside. The blocked holes allowed the mast to fill with rainwater until it overflowed through the diesel tank's breather pipe inside the mast.

Now that was a bit of a problem, because I thought the only way I could drain the water from the bottom of the diesel tank was by taking the boat out of the water. I needed to undo the bung and drain the water, which would sit at the bottom of the tank because it is heavier than diesel.

The first thing I needed to do was drill bigger holes in the bottom of the mast so the water could easily drain out, even if there was some dirt remaining. I'm not quite sure how dirt got in there, but I wondered if it might be the heads of pop rivets from when I was riveting various fittings onto the mast. The heads of the pop rivets could have fallen into the bottom of the mast, rolled across and blocked the holes.

I finally rigged up a hand pump to get rid of quite a bit of the water, but there was still some in the bottom of the fuel tank. Fortunately the pickup for the diesel was just high enough so it couldn't suck any more water into the motor, which was now running okay, but as soon as I got the opportunity I would take the boat out of the water and drain every last drop of water out of the tank.

We had a pretty good trip around the southern side of Viti Levu and eventually headed west to Musket Cove, our old stomping ground from five years earlier. We received a warm welcome from the locals who had become friends when we spent a whole year in Fiji.

We hadn't caught any fish for some time and out of sheer desperation I decided to set the net overnight by anchoring it at each end. In the morning the net was an absolute mess. We had caught a six-foot-long reef shark and a huge shark had cut it in two like a guillotine. The shark, probably a tiger shark or a great white, had also bitten right through the net and went on its way with the best part of the reef shark in its mouth. There were a number of other fish in the net so it took us quite a while to remove all of the fish and sew the net back together. It was absolute chaos, so we didn't set the net overnight there again.

We decided it wouldn't be a good idea to dive there any more, as tiger sharks grow to 16 feet long and are the most aggressive sharks in tropical waters. In all of my years of diving in the tropics, I have never encountered a tiger shark and I never want to.

Every year the Island Cruising NZ association organised a rally, sailing to either Tonga or Fiji. They left from Opua in the Bay of Islands and headed to Nadi on the western side of Fiji. The cruising rallies were very popular, with up to 30 yachts taking part.

I've never sailed up with the rally as I prefer to do my own thing, but it was often entertaining to listen on the radio to all the yachties competing for first place, even though it's not actually a race. There were often some very fast boats as well as quite slow boats, so it took a while for them all to gather in Fiji.

One of the highlights of the rally was the Musket Cove Regatta Week, which consisted of many yachts from all around the world converging on Musket Cove to take part in the festivities. They included a race around Malolo Island and stopping off at the Beachcomber Island Resort.

That race could become quite competitive and great fun, with possibly 50 or 60 yachts involved. It was quite spectacular, especially the first downwind leg of the race, with many colourful spinnakers flying.

Maxine *under spinnaker and mainsail during the fun race.*
Photo by B. McKeane

It could have been absolute chaos but fortunately the yachts sailed at very different speeds, so we spread out quickly. We got out the trusty spud gun and sneaked up on a couple of yachts we knew, managing to land the occasional spud on their decks or sails, much to their disgust. We were relieved that they didn't have spud guns to return fire.

Maxine finished the race in the middle of the field, not being a lightweight boat built for speed like some of the others.

Another highlight was the wet T-shirt competition, held on a beautiful beach on the far side of Malolo Island. The women wore very thin T-shirts and had a swim to get wet, then the judges could do their job, with great hilarity.

I had the onerous task of being a judge and discovered one of the few rules was that I wasn't allowed to touch. A magnifying glass could be used if necessary and you could measure things very carefully to determine the winner.

There were three categories: light displacement, medium displacement and heavy displacement. The judges always took their time making their decisions, which meant some contestants had to go for another swim to keep their T-shirts revealing enough.

They also ran a firm bum competition and the rules were quite different for that, because the female judges were all permitted to feel how firm those bums were. I thought that was a bit sexist but I put up with it, especially as I won. Someone accused me of putting a magazine inside my pants to make my bum feel firmer. Of course, the rules allowed them to take a look.

Next on the list was the hairy chest competition, which I didn't enter, not being well-endowed in that department. A good friend had a very hairy chest but when the judges seemed to lose interest, he removed his speedos and revealed an elephant's trunk with large ears attached to a g-string. Not surprisingly, he won.

It was then time for a big shared lunch on the beach with plenty of cold beer, followed by a race back to Musket Cove. Some of the skippers were a bit worse for wear by then, but the channel at Musket Cove was well marked.

Another really fun activity was the Hobie Cat races and some of the sailors took them very seriously. Unless they were very careful, they ended up flipping their Hobie Cats and losing the race. It was held in the large bay between Malolo Lailai and Malolo Island. We had to race around a triangular course and clear three buoys, and although my team didn't capsize we didn't place.

After all the competitions and hilarity, we gathered at the $2 Bar for the prize-giving and mixed with people from all over the world. Later we got out the guitars and had a huge sing-along.

This young crew member doesn't seem to mind all the lecherous sailors. Photo by J. Faulkner

Dick and Carol Smith did a great job organising the regatta for many years and their friendly staff went out of their way to be helpful. They carved the name of every boat that took part in the regatta in the main building's ceiling beams.

There were also plenty of activities for Jamie and Sam, with swimming races, egg-and-spoon races, three-legged races and all sorts of fun to keep them occupied.

Jamie and Sam entered the evening talent quest, performing Fred Dagg's "The Gumboot Song", wearing black singlets and oversized gumboots. Of course they won.

Jamie and Sam doing their thing. Note the sea boots. Photo by P. Faulkner

About 400 yachts entered Fiji that year, so we made new friends from many different countries. They enjoyed cruising on yachts of all sizes, from 26 to 100 feet.

I couldn't help reflecting on how independent and resilient these sailors were. They were from all walks of life, some very wealthy and some with very little.

One of the great things about Musket Cove was that we were on a mooring, so we didn't have to worry about dragging anchor. Every time we went somewhere we could just let go of our mooring instead of laboriously raising the anchor, then enjoy our daily adventures and just pick up the mooring on our return. Much more relaxing… We also didn't have to decide what to do each day because all of the activities were organised for us.

Musket Cove was very quiet at the end of the week. People were completely regatta'd out, so it was time to relax and laze by the pool. I was getting itchy feet and decided to head north towards the Yasawa Islands.

Our first stopover was at Mana Island, with another great swimming pool and children's playing areas, then we headed to Lautoka for water and provisions. Naturally we indulged ourselves again at the Snax Bar, chewed sugar cane at the mill and ate at our favourite Indian restaurant.

Then we set off for Octopus Resort on Waya Island, the southernmost island of the Yasawas. It had a very good anchorage in about 50 feet of water and a sandy bottom. Octopus Resort was a friendly place with a pool for Jamie and Sam to enjoy with the other children.

Sometimes we entertained ourselves by doing some boom swinging. I would push Jamie and Sam out on the main boom, drop them into the water, then they'd swim to the back of the boat and do it again. They could hold onto a rope on the boom, I would push it out really fast, then they would let go at the last minute and go flying out. It could be just a boom swing, if they wanted a gentle ride, but they never did. If they wanted a bit more action, I would take the boom up higher, swing them out and if they let go at the last minute they could do a bomb, or even a backflip.

One Monday morning, we visited the school. The children were a similar age to Jamie and Sam, and welcomed us with beautiful singing and some hilarious dances. We gave them exercise books, pens, pencils and rubbers, which they greatly appreciated.

We later anchored at Naukacuvu Island in Paradise Cove opposite the main resort and went ashore. The staff there were incredible and greeted us like old friends as they remembered us from last time we visited.

Jamie and Sam enjoyed the pool and we met the Australian crew from the other yacht, so several drinks followed. We made the most of the hot chips and burgers from the pool bar, which gave us a rest from cooking and dishes that night.

Our friends and their crew with us and a few locals. Photo by A. Wells

It was a lovely calm anchorage, in 50 feet of clear water with many fish jumping and strange birds calling from the rocky island behind us. The bay faced west, so we had an incredible sunset.

The pass at the far end of the island was famous for manta rays, so we snorkelled there the following morning. We saw four manta rays gliding through the pass, two of them huge, about 16 feet across, and just cruising along without a care in the world. The children were absolutely stunned by the size of them.

The coral in the pass was teeming with fish. The water streaming through the gap carried plenty of nutrients, so there were schools of tuna and mackerel and fish of all shapes, sizes and colours.

Making the most of the 15-knot southeasterly, we headed north to Nanuya Levu, about the midway point of the Yasawas. The lagoon was known as Blue Lagoon after the movie that was filmed there in 1980. Anchoring was a dream in the azure water and it was so clear we could see right to the bottom, where we dropped the anchor at 60 feet. There is a sandy point where the tide slowly slips away and you can lie in the lapping water as if you were on a beach chair. We watched the kids play in the shallows and it was like a postcard or a travel brochure.

The following day we went across to the Nanuya Resort shop for fresh fruit and veggies. They had pineapple and banana plantations, so that was a real treat. We asked at the store about crayfish and the next morning a couple of locals came along in their long boat to ask if we wanted to buy lobster. Obviously the grapevine worked well. We did some negotiating and eventually settled on a very fair price.

We headed to a spot where the nearby resort fed the fish daily and when the fish heard our engine they made a beeline for us. We fed bits of bread to hordes of fish, from tiny striped ones to big schools of brightly coloured parrot fish and everything in between. Jamie and Sam had to jump in and swim among them, while marvelling at those tame fish.

After three nights there, we headed to Yasawa Island, at the northernmost point, to check out the famous caves. We discovered it was going to cost $55 per person to go into the caves plus the cost of a guide, so we gave that a miss. We had already seen similar limestone caves in the Lau Group.

The wind was ideal for heading south and, as we had seen the islands on the way up, we decided to keep moving for a few days and just anchor overnight here and there. Our return trip south would have taken us around the east side of Waya, but it got rough, so we decided to pull in at Malakati Village on Nacula Island. It turned out to be a great decision, as it was an idyllic spot, and so we stayed for a couple of days.

This iguana made itself comfortable on my shoulder. Photo by J. Faulkner

One of the local children climbed a tree and brought us a beautiful green iguana. It was about a foot long and Sam wanted to keep it as a pet on the boat. The answer was a definite "no". He was disappointed, but we were able to see many different iguanas throughout the Yasawas.

There were also many different types of butterflies and Jamie was particularly taken by their spectacular colours and wore herself out trying to catch them.

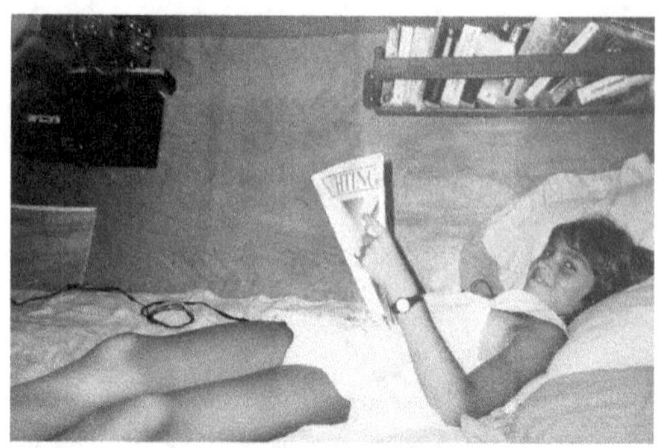

As Jamie was now getting quite tall, she sometimes preferred our cabin. Photo by P. Faulkner

The weather improved and we departed first thing in the morning, but the wind gradually got up again until it became very uncomfortable, so we turned west. We had missed a couple of islands on the way up and when we sailed into the protected bay of Natewa Island, we could see why it had been highly recommended.

There was a catamaran in the bay called *Double Trouble* and we felt sorry for them, as we had ruined their private anchorage, but when Jim and Helen paddled over with their three children, we felt very welcome.

We spent two of our most idyllic days there, with all of the children well entertained. There were hermit crabs to make crab hotels and have races with, as well as all of the usual beach activities. We had a huge bonfire on the beach with marshmallows and chocolate biscuits, as well as wine and beer for the adults.

Double Trouble was heading south as well, so we decided to sail together. Jamie and Sam were thrilled as they were constantly having to say goodbye to friends each time we moved.

We returned to the mainland and anchored at Denarau off the Regent Hotel and enjoyed their live music show while all the kids romped in the pool. We also wandered over to the nearby Sheraton to check out the entertainment and caught a bus into Nadi for movies and icecreams. Jill and I looked after all the children that night so Jim and Helen could have a rare date night at the Regent's nightclub.

We then headed further south to Robinson Crusoe Island, which shows up as Likuri Island on the charts, about seven miles southeast of Navula Passage, the main route to Western Fiji. There was room for about a dozen boats, as the owners, two retired Aussie couples, had put in free moorings to attract more yachts. They monitored VHF Channel 10 and happily sent out a boat to guide yachts in if required.

They had the best cultural show we had seen in Fiji, including knife dancing and fire dancing, as well as the more traditional performances. The staff obviously enjoyed putting the shows together and their enthusiasm was contagious.

Meals were only four dollars for a delicious buffet, which is a steal, as one of the owners also owned the local butchery. They did an excellent lovo lunch three times a week that was accompanied by a fire-walking and cultural show. The children were blown away by the Fijians walking on red-hot coals without any pain.

After three nights at Robinson Crusoe Island, we did a short hop back to Musket Cove, our home away from home. It was great to be back with all those familiar faces again. We did several excursions from there, before Jill and the children flew back to Auckland from Nadi.

My sister Jean and our nephews Kim and Eli flew in and I spent a few days showing them the highlights of some nearby islands. We then sailed home to Auckland together after stocking up on plenty of food to keep the ravenous teenagers happy.

I always felt a bit disoriented when I got back after a long sailing trip and found it difficult to adjust to the hustle and bustle of city life. I now had to decide what I was going to do next and I didn't really want to go back to selling houses. I decided to build another house, this time with my younger brother John and this took us about a year.

Over the next decade I did another two trips up to Fiji as I found that was the best location to sail to, compared with all the other Pacific Islands nearby. Fiji had all the facilities and parts for repairing the boat if needed, English was spoken everywhere and it was generally quite tidy and clean. The people are very easygoing and friendly and always welcomed us into their villages.

Also, I had made a number of friends there and it was great to catch up with them each time I went back. At one point I was invited to go into partnership in a dive operation and I would have done it as a lifestyle for a few years, but it was very difficult to have a business in Fiji as well as a yacht to look after. It would be too hard to do both, so I declined the offer.

My life took some big turns at that time and our marriage was not going very well. After 20 years together, Jill and I made the very difficult decision to divorce. It was also very hard on the children, but in the long run it was for the best.

My eldest brother Mike had built a yacht during this time and he was sailing in Tonga, so I decided to fly up and join him, his partner Carol and her son James. It was fun to spend a couple of weeks with them and do some cruising without the responsibility of looking after the boat for a change.

We were in the north of Tonga, in an area called Vava'u. One particular experience that I really enjoyed was sailing out to celebrate the opening of the Berlin Bar, which had just been built on a tiny island by a German couple. A talented keyboard player entertained us and I had my guitar, so we were able to play together. His keyboard was plugged into a car battery on the beach. It was one of those magical nights with a full moon, palms waving in a very gentle breeze and music until all hours of the night.

We had caught a tuna on our way to the island and thought it would be a welcome addition to the feast, but they already had three tuna. I've never seen so much sashimi, sushi and other tuna dishes. It's funny how sometimes special evenings just come together spontaneously like magic and I'll always remember that one.

The two weeks flew by and it wasn't long before I was back in Auckland yet again.

Chapter Nineteen

When I first started building *Maxine*, I made a pledge that if it ever got to the stage where I was working on the yacht more than I was sailing her, it was time to sell. That time had come, so I tidied her up, made her completely spick and span to go on the market, and it didn't take very long to sell her.

Many of my friends told me I would regret it, but it was a huge relief to not have to look after a boat any more. I also realised that after having the boat for 20 years and sailing on and off for 35 years, I felt like having some different adventures.

I was also aware of the fact that during most of my sailing adventures I only ever saw the edges of countries. I never saw the inland areas, so I decided it was time to change that and I headed off on a trip to Nepal to walk the Annapurna Circuit with my cousin Murray.

It was absolutely amazing to see such enormous mountains. Walking up a big river valley, we would come around a bend to be confronted by a huge mountain, way higher than we ever thought possible. There are eight mountains in Nepal almost as high as Everest.

We spent a lot of time hiking with Wolfgang from Germany and Richard from England, who just happened to be on the same schedule as us.

From left to right: Wolfgang, Murray, Richard and Wolfgang's porter Bikram. Photo courtesy of M. Faulkner

Occasionally we thought we were continuing along a river valley, when the trail suddenly started to climb in order to get around a gorge. Looking up I would see climbers way off in the distance, looking like ants and I realised that was how far I would have to climb. It was absolutely daunting.

These stone steps went on forever. Photo by S. Bartyzel

The climate kept changing. We started off at about 800 feet above sea level and, as we were near the equator, it was very hot. As we climbed higher and higher, the climate gradually became temperate and we saw apple and apricot trees. It felt very much like New Zealand. Climbing higher again, we got into really cold climate vegetation, then further on we were in bare rocks with huge eagles swooping over our heads.

Nothing much grew there, apart from a few sparse plants for the yaks to graze on. Those hardy animals can survive well at high altitude because of their long hair and extra-large lungs.

A domesticated yak. Photo by Y. Chaadeyev

At higher altitudes they are used to carry provisions as well as for their meat and milk. Yak cheese and butter are important staples, but the traditional yak butter tea is an acquired taste. Their wool is used for garments and their dung is vital for cooking fires because there are no trees at high altitude.

Yaks have large horns so we learned early on to give them a wide berth on the trail. They are not sacred animals in Nepal but are greatly revered and are often more colourfully decorated than the vibrant Sherpa women in traditional dress.

A feature of the trail was numerous swing bridges to cross the river, as the trail changed from one side to the other. This was necessary when the trail was blocked by a huge rock face.

A typical swing bridge high above a river. Photo by T. Tartes

While walking on some of the trails that had been carved out of solid rock, there was often a straight drop of several hundred feet down to the river. That was pretty scary and the most dangerous part of the journey was meeting a string of donkeys loaded with produce on a narrow part of the trail. Their loads protruded a long way on either side and as they didn't realise how wide they were, a donkey could inadvertently push someone over the edge. That has happened a few times. The lead donkeys wore bells around their necks, warning us to move to the inside of the trail. I often flattened myself into a recess in the cliff to let the donkeys pass safely.

There were often over 20 donkeys in a train. Photo by M. Faulkner

The locals were very friendly and everything was incredibly inexpensive. I ate mostly dal bhat, a lentil curry that was part of the local staple diet and served with rice or sometimes traditional flat bread. The two biggest advantages of eating dal bhat were the delicious taste and the fact that they had a tradition of refilling the dal bhat bowl until the guest was full. In my case, that took several refills and I didn't eat anything else on the menu, because the refill rule didn't apply to them.

My cousin Murray was like a mountain goat. He would sometimes walk almost twice the distance as he raced off in search of interesting mountain flora to satisfy his botanical curiosity. A few years later, to celebrate turning 70, he walked the length of New Zealand on the 1864-mile Te Araroa Trail.

Our incredibly strong Sherpa porter Nara, who carried most of our luggage, insisted on a strategy to avoid altitude sickness: Book into a tea house in the village that offered basic accommodation, take off our day packs and then climb about 200 feet higher. We would spend an hour there, taking in the view, then descend back to the village to spend the night in the teahouse at the slightly lower altitude.

A number of people have died in their sleep because they haven't used that acclimatisation technique. We slowed down a lot as we climbed higher and I was breathing as hard as if I was running just to get enough oxygen at that altitude. We eventually crossed over the Thorong La Pass at 17,769 feet and I found it very difficult. It took a lot out of us to keep going at that altitude as we weren't acclimatised to it. My nose bled and I had a headache and every step took a great effort, but it was amazing to be up so high in the snow.

We had made friends with a fit German called Wolfgang on the trail and he surprisingly succumbed to altitude sickness, so he had to ride a donkey over the pass.

Murray, Richard and me. We were all too exhausted to stand for this photo in front of the prayer flags at the summit. Photo courtesy of M. Faulkner

At 18,000 feet there is only half the amount of oxygen as at sea level and I was very pleased to descend again after a couple of days of only just being able to breathe enough to walk. We took 12 days to gradually get to that height in order to avoid altitude sickness, but after living at sea level all our lives, it would take a lot longer than that to get completely used to it.

In many ways, I found it harder on my legs descending than climbing. That was because all of my weight was pushed onto my knees with every step. Foolishly, I was keen to get down to a lower altitude quickly and tried to go too fast.

When we reached the end of the trail we stayed at a big lodge. Some of the friendly locals were dancing that night to traditional music. They had some very complicated dance moves and it was too difficult for us to join in, so we just enjoyed the cultural experience.

Our 19 days of hiking were over and we travelled to Pokhara by four wheel drive over a very rough road. We spent four days there, doing lots of sightseeing on bicycles.

We caught a bus to Chitwan National Park to look for tigers and rhino, choosing to walk rather than ride elephants. After seeing huge tiger prints and knowing that one had been sighted the day before, we felt very vulnerable on foot. The elephant grass was over eight feet high, so anything could have been lurking there.

A wide variety of monkeys entertained us as we searched for larger animals. When we found fresh rhino prints, our guide, who was heavily armed with a stick, suggested we climb a tree. It had a branch which leaned out and, very soon after we climbed onto it, a huge male rhino walked right under us. We could have jumped onto his back. After he wandered away, we continued our search for a tiger, sweating both from the heat and the fear of being pounced on at any moment. It was probably just as well there weren't any tigers around that day.

After a lengthy, torrid bus ride on potholed roads, we arrived back in Kathmandu and stayed in Durbar Square. It was in the old part of the city and was the best place to view traditional Nepalese architecture dating back to the 12th century. We climbed the steps of one temple and really enjoyed sitting near the top, while people watching.

There seemed to be lots of people watching the activities, including many locals. Photo by M. Faulkner

I didn't understand a lot of what was going on, but it was fascinating being immersed in another culture. A lot of activities had religious significance, mostly Buddhist. I heard a bizarre sound, almost like a didgeridoo, and followed it until I found a group playing very long horns, drums and a screechy stringed instrument. Apparently they were playing to keep bad spirits away. The raucous sound soon kept me away as well.

I enjoyed walking down the little alleyways where artisans were making pots, pans, touristy trinkets and bicycles. I found a silversmith and bought a little pendant made of silver and copper. In one of the squares, people were threshing wheat.

Photo by M. Faulkner

With such a huge population, they have to make the most of every space to do these chores.

Photo by M. Faulkner

After five weeks, it was time to head home again. It wasn't long before I was building yet another house, this time a house for me to live in behind a bungalow I had bought. I flatted with Carl Robson, a good friend of mine, while I built the house over a period of nine months. It was nice to move into a brand new house.

I got back into snow skiing, which I hadn't done for many years and really enjoyed that. I had also tried hang gliding when I was younger and decided to have another go. It was exhilarating being up so high and flying like a bird. I could stay up there for hours, ridge soaring along the North Island West Coast with friends then landing on the beach.

I also took up Ceroc dancing and immersed myself in it for a few years, even doing some competition dancing. I really loved dancing, but I had to drag myself out to dance classes after an exhausting day building.

I met Annmarie at one of those dance classes and we got on really well and started seeing quite a lot of each other. I talked about my sailing experiences and she mentioned that she would love to do that, so I suggested we sail to Fiji.

We joined the South Pacific Cruising Rally and put our names down to crew on somebody's yacht. We managed to get a position on a 48-foot yacht out of Sydney, with Sandy and Claire from England and the two owners from Sydney.

The six of us set off on the annual cruising rally to Fiji and had a fairly uneventful trip up over eight days.

The boat was very easy to sail as it had all sorts of electronics, including an electrically operated main sail. So it was very comfortable and great fun sailing with such a good crew. Annmarie really enjoyed it and Sandy and Claire were great fun to be around. We just enjoyed each other's company.

The rally organisers arranged for Customs and Immigration to clear us in at Kadavu, which is a very large island 70 miles south of Suva. There were a lot of festivities, barbecues and partying.

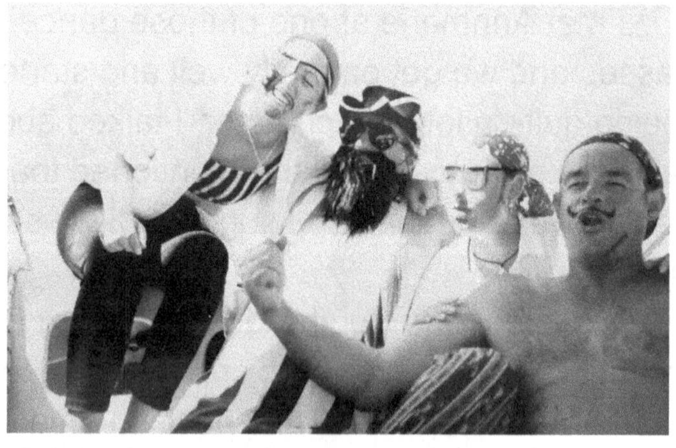

Four larrikins enjoying the festivities. What a great crew!

I joined a guided scuba diving trip to the other side of the island where there were some giant manta rays. They were absolutely amazing. We got down to about 90 feet and, as we were coming up, huge manta rays were just gliding above us like spaceships.

They were probably around 12 feet across and very gentle. It was amazing to see their horns, as we called them, which protruded out in front. They uncurled to form a big funnel and scooped up plankton as the rays swam along. Some of the coral there was spectacular, so it was a very memorable dive.

The owners of the boat had some family arriving, so we talked to the owners of *Foxy Lady II,* from Wellington, who were also in the regatta, and they were happy to have us on board as crew.

It wasn't long before we were back at Musket Cove, where I hadn't expected to return after selling *Maxine.* It was great to be back there again and we had a whole week of madness with the Musket Cove Regatta Week, joining in all the fun and we actually came second in the Hobie Cat races.

Inventing outfits for the dress-up party was a fun challenge. I dressed as a "piss head", with a beer box on my head.

Annmarie, Sandy, Claire and me

The time just flew by and it wasn't long before a week was over. We had one week left to explore some of the islands in the southern Yasawa Group before flying back to Auckland.

Chapter Twenty

    When I got back to Auckland I had plenty to do, as I was in the middle of finishing the very large house, primarily on my own. I had decided that I didn't want to work for anybody else again and if I could finish that house and sell it for the right price, I could retire.

    In my 50s and keen to move out of Auckland, I was looking at properties in the Bay of Plenty without any success. When I was halfway through building the house, Annmarie's brother suggested a short-term project for me. He was working on an aquarium on the island of Mallorca, Spain, as a builder.

    They were looking for more builders and as I had done quite a lot of work with timber, they offered me a three-month contract. That was a good opportunity for a change of scenery, so off I went.

It was winter in Mallorca, thankfully, with very cool mornings, but it was reasonably hot in the afternoons. The aquarium project was huge, spanning 15 acres, and it was to be the largest aquarium in Europe. The department I was working in was responsible for beautification and setting the scene in the aquarium.

My first job was making timber walkways through the rainforest area and doing lots of creative work with bamboo.

The walkway, which would meander down through the forest.
Photo by P. Faulkner

The timber we used was very heavy and had been cut to look old and rustic. The timber walkway started at a height of about 40 feet and meandered its way down to ground level, which would enable visitors to view the rainforest from many angles.

Another project was attaching plastic four-by-four-inch planks to a concrete wall to make a hanging garden. That involved running irrigation pipes along each section, then attaching plastic mesh and fixing layers of coconut fibre to that. Plants were inserted into the fibre and effectively disguised the concrete wall.

In the rainforest section I was involved in building branches to come out the top of huge ficus trees. The company had made moulds of rainforest trees when they were building their previous aquarium in Malaysia.

It was fun sitting right up on top of those trees about 30 feet high and then building steel branches coming out on various sides. They supported wire mesh with ferro-cement coating, to make them look like real branches growing out of the fibreglass trees.

There was also a massive pump to circulate fresh water to form the 40-foot-high waterfall. It seemed a bit bizarre, but in the end it worked out very well and the trees looked very much in keeping with a tropical rainforest.

There were also many rock walls, which had been fabricated in the same method using steel frames and a ferro-cement finish to give the impression of Inca walls.

My boss, Simon, who was also a Kiwi, asked if I knew anything about stainless steel welding. He knew that I had built a couple of yachts, so he put my skills to a strange use – building rocks to go in the main aquarium tank. Those massive rocks had layers and holes through the layers to make them look like real rocks when they were underwater.

I would make a stainless steel frame strong enough to hold the whole thing up, and then the next team would come in and cover the frame with plastic mesh. Another team would spray coat it with the ferro-cement mixture and colour them to look authentic underwater with anemones and other things growing on them.

People would come along and wonder what on earth I was doing, but Simon was happy with my first rock frame. He let me design the next one, so it was fun making up natural looking shapes and all the holes for fish to swim through, as I had seen many times while diving.

They were very large and the first one weighed around a ton. It had to be lifted up and lowered through the main aquarium's open roof, then set in place.

Simon and our first big rock being lifted into position. Photo by P. Faulkner

I was living in quite a nice hotel directly over the road from the aquarium and would call in at a little shop to buy fresh baguettes for a leisurely lunch at home.

At Christmas time Annmarie and her daughter Elsa came over for a few weeks and we did a trip to the mainland. We hired a car and drove to Seville, which is reputedly the hottest city in Europe, and even in midwinter it was pretty warm.

We were absolutely enthralled by the architecture of the Alcazar Palace with its stunning gardens.

We also travelled to Granada and enjoyed the gardens and Moorish architecture at the

Alhambra Palace. I was astounded by the intricate artwork, using tiny mosaic tiles over huge areas.

It was surprising to see a lot of snow on the surrounding Sierra Nevada mountains after being mostly in hot places.

We had a great holiday, just tripping around various places in the south of Spain and trying out the tapas bars and small restaurants, especially in the traditional old villages.

After two weeks I was back at work. I had been away longer than I was supposed to, but I managed to get away with it. I was really enjoying my job and got to know some of the management team, who showed me around the aquarium.

I was keen to learn about all the technical aspects of running the aquarium. They showed me how the filtration systems and pumps worked, pumping sea water from the local beach and obviously filtering everything very carefully.

They were also catching fish in the Mediterranean and I was pretty keen to go out diving with them. Unfortunately I couldn't take any more time off my job because I was very busy building all sorts of things and making up for the time I had spent touring around.

A couple of times after work, we sat around and had a few beers and one of the workers was a very good Spanish guitarist. We had a few jams together, which was fun.

I heard that Jose Carreras was performing in the cathedral in Palma and there was no way I was going to miss his concert. It was only for locals, so there were no door sales and tickets could only be sent to a home address.

I just lined up in the queue, not knowing how I was going to get in without a ticket. The queue went around a couple of city blocks and I kept slowly moving forward until I got to the front.

Everyone was speaking Spanish excitedly and I didn't understand a word.

At the door, they said, "If you have no ticket you can't go in. Just stand over there." A man who was behind me in the queue overheard that and said, "I have a spare ticket. Would you like it?"

That was a huge relief and I got a really good seat in the middle, quite well forward. The acoustics in the cathedral were absolutely stunning and to hear someone as good as Jose Carreras was just such a treat. I will always remember that.

My boss Simon and his wife Vicky sometimes took me for a drive around the island and showed me where they lived. Some of the workers lived in the country and they would invite us out for a traditional Spanish meal, which was very generous.

On one occasion we visited Juan and his parents, who lived in a gorgeous old stone house with a big cellar. Juan's father made wine, which we sampled with our lunch.

I asked if I could buy some and he only charged me 20 euros for a large container of great quality wine. There was far too much for me to drink, but my new friends enjoyed sharing it.

Sampling the delicious red wine on the side of the road.

The people on Mallorca were quite different from the Spanish people on the mainland. They had a different dialect and although I didn't speak Spanish I could hear that they sounded different. They were very laidback and many of them lived quite a traditional lifestyle.

Almost everything was built out of rock, so most of the local builders weren't familiar with building in timber and that was how I got the wonderful opportunity to work there.

It was fascinating to wander around the marina checking out the huge expensive looking yachts and power boats. I would try to imagine the lifestyle of the people who owned them.

Most of the shops were closed over the winter and the owners just pulled down big garage doors over the shop fronts and went away on holiday.

It was quiet then and the beaches were virtually empty. I heard that in the summertime the beach was completely covered in umbrellas and people, with hardly a patch of sand visible. Over 12 million visitors come to Mallorca every summer. The jets must be landing every minute, bringing passengers in constantly.

Even in winter the planes were coming regularly, lining up and circling in midair waiting for their landing slots. Despite all that activity, there weren't enough winter tourists to fill all of the apartments and hotels, and so many of them closed completely for a few months.

My three-month contract went by very quickly and I was asked to stay on and do another three months, but I was itching to get back and finish the house and so declined their offer, but thanked them profusely for inviting me to work there on such an interesting and creative project.

My only regret was that I didn't get to see the aquarium when it was completed and full of fish.

Chapter Twenty-One

Back in Auckland, I thought it would take about three months to finish the house. Everything about it was big, with four large bedrooms, two bathrooms and a huge 1000-square-foot family room, dining and kitchen area. It had a hardwood timber floor on top of concrete and my knees did not appreciate laying down that big area.

After 12 months of hard work I finally finished it and eventually sold it for quite a good price, although I discovered that the prices went through the roof later on. I could have made a lot more money if I'd had a crystal ball, but I wasn't too concerned because I had enough money to retire on.

I still had the old bungalow in front and it badly needed renovating, so that was to be my last big job in Auckland. I remember showing the bungalow to my son Sam and he said, "Even a student wouldn't live in this dump." I took out walls and built a new kitchen, along with a new en suite and a new bathroom, plus a lot of painting and fixing up. The finishing touch was a beautiful macrocarpa benchtop, which I finished with a clear epoxy coating and it looked quite stunning. The bungalow was at last finished.

I wasn't ready to sell the house yet, so I decided to rent it to Sam and a couple of his friends at a very low rental, since it was now up to his high standards.

Now that I had more spare time, I decided to have a more serious look at properties to buy in the Bay of Plenty. I finally found a property that I liked on the Tauranga Harbour near Katikati.

The house, which didn't need any work, stood on one acre of beautiful gardens and I knew immediately it was the one. I was tired of doing up houses at that point and just wanted somewhere to enjoy life. I also chose the property because of the good growing conditions and excellent soil. The house was surrounded by good shelter trees and an organic kiwifruit orchard. Being by the harbour also meant I could catch flounder close to the house.

I had become more involved in the Auckland music scene, attending the Devonport Folk

Music Club and listening to all sorts of different musicians. I wasn't really into folk music, but there were few venues with live, acoustic music. I played there occasionally and also went quite regularly to a jam night at The Thirsty Dog, a pub in Auckland's red light district on Karangahape Road.

I had been going there for two years and several musicians would sit around a table and take turns leading a song. The others would join in and the jam session had a very inclusive atmosphere. We played many different styles of music and sometimes sang a capella.

Occasionally some very experienced musicians came along. I really enjoyed playing "Closing Time" by Lyle Lovett and sometimes a top violinist joined in, playing a great solo in the middle of the song. It was fun improvising with all of the different musicians who turned up.

Family and friends sometimes came to listen, in particular my brother John, my sister Jean and my cousin Murray. David Bott also came regularly and one evening he said, "I've seen a yacht that you just have to buy!" I told him I had finished with sailing, but he insisted that this 34-foot Spencer Saraband was a steal at only $6000. I knew it was a very good design and thought it sounded too good to be true, so of course I couldn't resist having a look while it was on the dry dock at the Panmure Yacht Club.

There was no glass in the windows and water in the bilge. The yacht was a neglected mess, but the owner said there was a brand new mainsail, new rigging and upholstery and the diesel motor had been completely overhauled. He also had a lot of other useful boating items at home that he would include in the sale. This was too good an opportunity to miss, so I bought her.

Even though I wasn't really keen on doing more sailing, I decided it was a worthwhile project. I stayed in Auckland for another three months working on *Maxine II,* as I renamed her, and continued going to the jam sessions at The Thirsty Dog. One night I noticed a very good singer and I was attracted to her smile and her beautiful voice. After that, Jacquie and I would often sit next to each other and chat away and sing and play. Eventually she went on a trip to the Galapagos Islands and I discovered that I really missed her.

When she returned, I asked her out on an unusual first date. I said, "Would you like to come and help me put my mast up?" Some people chuckled at that suggestion, especially Jacquie's mother, but she said yes.

Jacquie came out to the yacht and we were just about to set off from the jetty when David arrived. She breathed a sigh of relief, knowing that David would know a lot more about putting a mast up.

We went down the river to another yacht club that had a really good gantry for lifting the mast. It was quite an ordeal and took longer than I expected to get the mast up and the rigging tensioned. Jacquie said she enjoyed being involved in the whole process and watching David and I working through all the problems that cropped up.

It was lucky that David turned up as he was experienced and Jacquie told me that she struggled to follow all the instructions and hold the lines tight enough. I had underestimated how much strength and skill was required for that job, but she really enjoyed being involved.

It was much more interesting than going out for a coffee and we got to know each other better while doing something completely different.

We all had great fun sailing back up the harbour together after the mast was up at last.

Jacquie and I started spending a lot of time together and I soon realised Jacquie was going to be my forever partner. We are both very grateful to David for making me buy that yacht.

I bought a mooring at Omokoroa and David helped me sail *Maxine II* from Auckland to Tauranga. She sailed surprisingly well and was a lot lighter and more responsive than the boats I was used to sailing offshore. She still needed a bit of work and I could do that on the mooring, so there was really nothing holding me in Auckland.

I moved down to the Bay of Plenty and invited Jacquie down for a weekend. She fell in love with the place and that was that. We were a team, never to be parted.

We went out for a few sailing trips to nearby islands as I gradually taught Jacquie how to sail, which she found very confusing at first. She would be trying to steer with the tiller while following my instructions:

"Pull the red line! No, not that one! The other red one!"

Of course, if she needed both hands to control the tiller, it was impossible to pull anything, so she said, "Do you want me to use my teeth?!"

Jacquie steered while I swanned around taking photos.

There was a lot to learn, but we both enjoyed being out on the water. The next summer we decided to go on a more extended holiday and took the boat up the coast to the Mercury Islands, then on to Arid Island and Great Barrier Island, which I had visited many times before.

Maxine II *at anchor. Photo by P. Faulkner*

It was fun catching up with a few of my friends who lived there, especially Alan Phelps, who invited us to his cafe for New Year's Eve. I took the guitar and we played music in return for drinks and meals. He picked us up from the boat and dropped us back late that night, by which time I had drunk a few too many beers.

It was pitch dark and we didn't have a torch, so we stumbled our way down the muddy bush track and somehow got the dinghy into the water. Then it was a matter of trying to find the yacht in the bay with no lights. We eventually found the yacht and Jacquie was amazed that I climbed up onto *Maxine II* without damaging my precious guitar. That old Yamaha guitar has survived many adventures with me and is in surprisingly good condition.

We spent about a month sailing around Great Barrier, exploring all the different bays and doing lots of diving. It was great to see Jacquie enjoying it so much.

Jacquie peering out from under the cockpit bimini. Photo by P. Faulkner*

During our trip home we caught a tuna that would provide quite a few meals. We had a great sail and the wind dropped off just before we entered the Tauranga Harbour. A huge cruise ship was coming out, so we waited until we were well clear of that.

My brother Mike was skipper on a large patrol boat there that was protecting the wreck of the *Rena* container ship near Tauranga. He had the night off, so we joined him at the marina for fish and chips and stayed overnight in the harbour, enjoying the constant clatter of container ships being unloaded.

The next morning, while motoring back to Omokoroa in torrential rain, we came across a large pod of orca. A huge male came straight towards our boat and his dorsal fin was eight feet out of the water. At the last possible moment he dived and then popped up behind us.

There was a guy paddling a kayak nearby, concentrating hard with his head down. He was totally oblivious to the fact that he was surrounded by huge orca. It was amazing to have such a close encounter with those gigantic creatures and they certainly brightened that stormy day.

After we had been home for a while, we realised that we didn't have enough time for sailing. We spent more time maintaining *Maxine II* than sailing her and so I managed to sell her very quickly to someone who had been looking for a Spencer Saraband with bilge keels for some time.

Jacquie and I had many other interests in common, like music, gardening and overseas travel. We were establishing vegetable gardens, planting lots of fruit trees and removing many overgrown ornamental trees. I also wanted to take Jacquie skiing and I was teaching her how to dance ceroc.

Our music duo, *Two's Company,* was keeping us busy with an increasing number of gigs away from home.

Two's Company NZ Music Duo promo photo. Photo by J. Logan

Annual winter music tours were a great way to play music together, catch up with family and friends and ski in the South Island.

I started writing songs, which I had never tried before, and learned how to record in my home studio. That was very difficult as I had hardly used a computer apart from sending emails.

Eventually, with a lot of help from friends and family and many hours in the studio, I managed to record enough originals and covers to make CDs and share songs on YouTube.

We changed our duo's online name, because typing in "Two's Company" brings up a lot of dating agencies, and so we became "Two's Company NZ Music Duo".

One Christmas, while holidaying with our family in Ohope, my nephew Tim took pity on us and kindly set up a Facebook page so we could interact with our followers.

Chapter Twenty-Two

In 2012, we got married in Jacquie's family's beautiful garden in Ramarama, south of Auckland.

Jacquie's mother Wendy with us at our wedding. Photo by Celeste Stark

With Jamie and Sam. Photo by Celeste Stark

We had many 'honeymoons' and the first was a canoe trip on the Yukon River in Canada. We did ski trips in Japan and Oregon and a wonderful campervan trip in Namibia, as well as great camping and hiking trips in New Zealand. We both have cousins in the United States, so we visited them and hiked in some huge national parks: Denali, Yosemite and Yellowstone.

My son Sam married Leliane in Brazil, so that gave us a wonderful excuse to go there, with a side trip to Cuba.

Jacquie and Jamie listening to a great Cuban band in a superb old hotel in Havana. Photo by P. Faulkner

My daughter Jamie married Marcus in Samoa and we enjoyed being back in the beautiful South Pacific for a few days.

We got interested in cycling, after one of our neighbours told us about her cycling trip in

Europe. So, we did three cycling trips. Serbia and Romania along the Danube River to the Black Sea, France along the Loire River, then on to the Meuse River to Belgium and Holland.

Having a rest in a beautiful forest in Holland. Photo by P. Faulkner

We met some New Zealand friends in Holland and hired a boat to explore some of the waterways in Friesland.

We then cycled from Zurich to the Camargue in France, then up the Midi and Garonne canals to Bordeaux. Cycling allowed us to travel slowly, with the freedom to stop and camp wherever we wanted. We usually covered about 45 miles per day, but there was no set itinerary.

Me about to do a nose-dive into the lake on a hot day in Belgium. Photo by J. Faulkner

After all the sailing I had done, it was a huge change to travel on land, but I still liked to go at a slow pace and tried to find quieter places to stop. Even in Europe we sometimes managed to find those by camping whenever possible. My sailing days were over, but I knew that there were so many other great ways to explore the world.

Both of my children have done a lot of travelling too, and my son Sam now lives in London. I asked him for his impressions of growing up on the boat:

"I know I spent a lot of my early childhood growing up on a boat in the South Pacific. I've seen the photos! For the very early years, I can't really distinguish between my own memories from being there, and things people have told me as I got older… I feel like I can remember falling into the ocean in Fiji when I was two years old,

but that can't be my own memory – I really just remember my dad telling me the story.

"The things I definitely remember seem to involve fish! We would set a nylon-mesh fishing net around sunset in a likely channel near the bay we anchored in for the night. At first light my dad would throw me a gigantic raincoat and sit me on the cold aluminium seat of our dinghy. I can still feel the excitement and anticipation, pulling up the net; watching as flashes of silvery scales began to reflect the light near the surface. Sometimes we would end up with a half-eaten fish.

"Living on a boat there were always physical tasks that I was eager to 'help' with, despite being small. My favourite was to try and start the motor on the dinghy (a failure if not done on the first attempt!). Others included: pulling on a rope when we were sailing, tying off a fender when coming into a marina or steering the boat while we moved from one bay to another. This would be the equivalent of pressing the button at a street crossing for a city kid. Often these tasks would need to be done under stressful conditions, like the boat leaning over and things falling from cupboards.

"There is nowhere to hide on a small boat! Our entire home was only 12 metres long, and my sister and I shared a very small cabin. We did our correspondence school lessons, ate all our meals, and generally lived in an area that would barely qualify as a lounge in a very small house. Living in close proximity sometimes led to 'cabin fever', particularly when it rained for a few days and we were stuck inside.

"Sometimes my sister and I would fight, leading to our parents needing to separate us. I started reading books as a way to pass the time and still read a lot today. Inevitably the sun would come out again and we could be entertained by snorkelling, spear fishing, trips ashore to a nearby island and playing with kids from the village.

"As an adult, I sometimes wonder how my dad built the boat we lived on all by himself. Floating on a small piece of steel in the middle of the Pacific Ocean hundreds of kilometres from land is scary. When you are in a bad storm and thinking about whether you assembled the thing correctly, it must be terrifying.

"On the odd occasion I end up on a boat nowadays I notice how I never seem to get sea sick, that the movement feels strangely familiar, *and that I can keep my balance fairly well. I don't, however, have a strong desire to go island hopping in the tropics. It was a special part of my childhood but feels like a memory I don't want to try and replicate – it could never quite be the same."*

Here are Jamie's impressions of yacht life:

"When I tell someone that I lived on a yacht, sailing around the South Pacific, they tend to react with awe: 'Wow, what an amazing childhood. How did that come about? How could you afford it? Weren't you lonely!?'

"My dad is a free-spirited nomad. He always has one foot in the present and one in the sea or planning his next adventure. I didn't think there was anything unusual about this lifestyle. Oysters were as common as chicken for dinner.

"We often met new kids and would sometimes cruise around with other yachting families.

Although my brother Sam and I were young for most of this time, I still have some vivid memories. Namotu is an island near the famous surfing spot called Cloudbreak. We were snorkelling one day when a reef shark came into the vicinity. I was keen on swimming with it but Mum freaked out and made us get out of the water. We later learned that this reef shark was a local named George and pretty harmless.

"A scary time was when we were motoring through the channel near Denarau. Dad was up the mast sitting on a spreader spotting coral bommies. Mum and Sam were below deck and I was steering. Suddenly we hit something and stopped dead. Dad nearly fell off the mast and my mum ended up with a huge bruise on her hip from banging into the table. I don't think I steered again after that. Dad tried to convince me it wasn't my fault. Apparently the sea wasn't as clear as usual, due to the Nadi River bringing in muddy water, so Dad didn't see one of the bommies.

"We had a children's inflatable dinghy for a while and one day our parents kicked us out to go paddling in the rain. We were jumping out and climbing in and we were both in the water when this huge mass rose up next to us. Scrambling for the dinghy, we reached safety only to realise it was an enormous curious turtle coming to say hello.

"My dad is New Zealand's version of Tim the Toolman Taylor. He can DIY anything. His sheds are full of bits and pieces; all very organised… he says he knows where everything is. He taught *himself how to build a boat before YouTube existed, how to build houses, how to play the guitar and then to record, edit and produce music. He built his own torpedo fishing rig, fruit and vegetable dehydrator, wine cellar out of a shipping container, bikes from parts and a kick drum. And so many other things that it would take another book to describe them. He would tinker with the tractor engine in the boat and the dinghy motor every time it broke down. I thought there was nothing my dad couldn't do and if he ever encountered something he couldn't fix, he always had beer or wine or fruit to trade with someone who could.*

"Looking back on the life Dad has led, I can't help but feel like I have not lived up to him. I'm really proud of my dad, all he achieved, the man he is and the incredible strength he has to get through the toughest of times, still with a cheeky sense of humour and a smile on his face."

After reading Jamie and Sam's words, I realise that if I had my time over again, I wouldn't change a thing in terms of all the time and energy I invested in ocean adventures and building boats. Talking to friends and family, I realised that when they joined me on some of my sailing adventures, it had a huge impact on their lives. For example my friend John Newton said:

"I've never felt so miserable, but had such a good time, all on the same trip. It was one of the great experiences of my life, up there with hiking to Base Camp on Everest."

My love of being on the water started at the age of six, building corrugated iron canoes with my brothers to use on a small lake on our farm. Later, my father and eldest brother included me on their fishing trips, so their love of the sea was contagious and perhaps inherited, as my great, great, grandfather was a Norwegian boatbuilder.

What drove me was mainly the satisfaction of building a seaworthy boat capable of huge adventures.

While writing about my sailing life, I reflected on how it gave me a rare opportunity to really get to know my crews well, as we were confined close together in an environment almost free of distractions. In the process, I learned a lot about myself and realised that if I thought I knew it all, the next crashing wave would remind me that I still had a lot to learn.

I was never completely in charge because I could 'master a boat, but never the sea'.

I think the famous racing sailor Sir Ben Ainslie, with all of his vast experience, summed it up best when he said:

"The simple pleasure of enjoying a boat moved along by wind is satisfaction at an elementary level. Good company on a boat is one of the best ways of chilling out that I know."

<u>Glossary</u>

<u>Beam reach</u>: When the wind is hitting the boat from behind and slightly off to one side at a slight angle of 130 to 150 degrees.

<u>Bimini:</u> A metal frame covered in canvas to make a roof over the cockpit, mainly for protection from the sun.

<u>Broach</u>: When a boat goes side-on to the waves and leans hard over. This has the potential to be disastrous in heavy seas.

<u>Chine</u>: A corner on the hull where the bottom plate meets the side plate. This corner is not present on a round bilge boat, where all of the steel plates are rolled to a compound curve by specialised machines.

<u>Cutter rig</u>: A yacht with a forestay and an inner forestay.

<u>Dodger</u>: A metal frame covered with canvas to protect the entry hatch and occupants of the cockpit against wind and spray. This can also be made of fibreglass or plywood.

<u>Flopper stopper</u>: A passive stabilisation device attached to the end of either the main boom or a jib pole. It uses a large steel frame with steel doors that open when the boat rolls to one side, then close when the boat tries to roll

back the other way. This is to prevent an uncomfortable roll from side to side while at anchor.

Forestay: The rigging wire at the front of a yacht.

Gaff: An aerial spar called a gaff holds aloft a four-cornered sail.

Genoa: A big lightweight headsail.

Gib® board: A board also known as wallboard, plasterboard or drywall and used for lining the interior of a house.

Grid: A set of poles that the boat is firmly tied to at high tide so when the tide goes out, the boat leans safely against the poles. This allows for work to be done on the hull below the waterline.

Gybing: Changing from one side of the wind to the other while sailing downwind.

Head sail (see jib)

Jib: A sail attached to the rigging wires in front of the mast (also called a headsail). Depending on the size, they are called number one jib, number two, etc.

Jib pole: see whisker-pole.

Ketch: A two-masted sailing vessel with a main mast and a shorter mast located forward of the rudder post.

Leeboard: A form of pivoting keel used by a sailboat and often used in lieu of a fixed keel. These are typically mounted in pairs on each side of a hull.

Loom: The light that can sometimes be seen from a lighthouse that is over the horizon, due to the light being scattered upward by water vapour particles.

Luff: The front edge of the sail.

Mainsail or main: The sail behind the mast.

Mainsail sheet: The rope attached to the bottom of the main via the boom. It controls the tension of the mainsail depending on the wind direction.

Painter: The rope used to tie a dinghy to the back of a boat or a jetty.

Roller furling: An aluminium tube that the front edge of the headsail or jib is attached to. This rotates around the forestay and enables the size of the headsail to be easily reduced or increased by pulling the roller furling sheet.

Self-steering gear:

A wind vane that rotates on a vertical axis like a weathercock and is linked to a small trim tab attached to the aft (or trailing) edge of the rudder, like the flap on a plane's wing. When the boat is on course, the wind vane is set so its leading edge points into the wind and offers no resistance. When the boat veers off course, the wind vane presents its side to the wind, which then pushes it around its axis, and this movement is transferred by linkage to the trim-tab, which, like the wing flap, moves the entire rudder and steers the boat back onto its original course. Normally, this gear is attached to a boat's stern, directly over the rudder.

<u>Sheet</u>: A rope attached to the bottom outer corner of a head sail. It is run back to a winch in order to tighten and loosen the sail.

<u>Stanchion</u>: A vertical stainless steel post to which handrail wires are attached to make a fence around the deck.

<u>Stay</u>: A stainless steel wire holding the mast up.

<u>Storm jib</u>: A small heavy headsail/jib for use in very strong winds over 40 knots.

<u>Sumlog</u>®: A distance measuring device. This small nylon propellor is mounted under the boat and turns a cable attached to a dial to show the speed and distance travelled. The level of accuracy is affected by the direction of currents: if travelling against the current, the distance shown will be greater and vice versa when travelling with the current.

Tacking: Changing from one side of the wind to the other while sailing upwind.

Whisker-pole: A long pole holding the headsail or jib as far out to one side as it will go, for running downwind (also called a jib pole).

Wing and wing: For sailing downwind, when you have one sail poled out to port and one to starboard, they look like a bird's wings. This is more stable than having the mainsail out one side and a headsail out the other.